Praise for Erwin Lutzer and
He Will Be the Preacher

I have to admit, I was humbled to be asked to endorse a book by Erwin Lutzer.

Yes, his life has been greatly impacted by my father, Billy Graham, and I understand and appreciate that fact; however, Daddy, who greatly admires Dr. Lutzer, would want all glory given to God for any influence he had on his life.

I have been truly blessed reading this book. It tells a simple yet profound story of how one man was chosen by God, even from his cradle, to be a preacher. It shows how he was available to the leadings of the Holy Spirit, and how ordinary choices and decisions have shaped his life. How overcoming many obstacles, including extreme shyness, didn't deter him from his calling.

What an encouragement to all men and women, young and old, to be reminded of how God leads His dear children along. Dr. Lutzer is not only a "great preacher," but because of his gentle spirit and deep compassion he is also a "true pastor."

I am privileged to call him my friend.

GIGI GRAHAM
Daughter of Billy and Ruth Graham

We have an extraordinary God who uses regular people. From a humble beginning, God has raised up Erwin Lutzer to impact the world for Christ through one of the most recognized pulpits on earth. By His grace and through many challenging seasons, God refined and used this man. Read *He Will Be the Preacher* to be stirred with fresh passion to follow our Sovereign God.

DR. JAMES MACDONALD
Founding pastor of Harvest Bible Chapel
Bible teacher on *Walk in the Word*

Drawing on decades of life and faithful gospel ministry, this memoir offers seasoned wisdom and encouragement for followers and servants of Christ. Dr. Lutzer reflects on his journey, including marriage and family, influences and opportunities, failures and regrets, losses sustained and lessons learned—with grateful recognition of the grace and providential hand of God through it all.

NANCY LEIGH DEMOSS
Author and teacher/host of *Revive Our Hearts*

D1041920

An autobiography written by a Christian can be a dangerous feat to attempt. However, this one highlights the God of the man behind the man of God who wrote it. The life story of my friend Pastor Erwin Lutzer is informative for its history, inspiring by its example, and even instructive for anyone serving in ministry or contemplating an obedient response to God's call to a lifetime of faithful service.

MARK L. BAILEY
President, Dallas Theological Seminary

Dr. Erwin Lutzer's *He Will Be the Preacher* offers an inside look at how God can take a timid young man from a farming background and lead him to become one of the most influential ministers in America. Readers will be encouraged and inspired by the story and impact of a life well lived for the glory of God.

DR. JOHN ANKERBERG
President and host of *The John Ankerberg Show*

I love biographies, and that's why I was excited when Erwin gave me his autobiography to read! I had yet more to learn from this man who has been a dear friend and counselor over the years.

The three words in this book that describe the value of reading Erwin's story are, *"I asked God."* If you want to know what it is like to "ask God" about anything and everything, from finding a parking space and a mate to the wheres and hows of ministry, valuing your wife when you're not on the same page, fighting crippling emotions, lawsuits, ministering in an antagonistic culture with the love of Christ, and so much more, then this is a book you don't want to miss! I've been discipled!

KAY ARTHUR
Cofounder, Precept Ministries International

Erwin Lutzer is as gifted a writer as he is a communicator. Pastor Lutzer's passion to proclaim the transforming power of the gospel with clarity and boldness, in a variety of contexts over many years, is instructive for all of us, and arguably his greatest legacy. It was a privilege to serve as executive pastor with him for seven years, but I am even more grateful to call Erwin my friend for many more.

HUTZ H. HERTZBERG
Senior Protestant chaplain, Chicago O'Hare and Midway Airports
Former executive pastor, The Moody Church

I'm so grateful for the powerful testimony of my friend Pastor Lutzer. His book will encourage you to look at God's providence in your life as he shares his very inspiring faith journey with you.

WILFREDO "CHOCO" DE JESÚS
Senior pastor, New Life Covenant Church, Chicago
Author of *In the Gap* and *Amazing Faith*

Every life touched by the grace of God has a story. A story that includes thirty-five years as pastor of the historic Moody Church is exceptional. I thank God for the faithful and powerful ministry of Dr. Erwin Lutzer. His unusual but divinely directed journey provides timely insight and wisdom for each follower of Jesus. Enjoy. Reflect. Rejoice.

J. Paul Nyquist
President, Moody Bible Institute

Dr. Lutzer has been an incisive Bible teacher and gospel apologist for decades. But often the best messages are *life messages*. In this book Dr. Lutzer shares warmly and transparently about pastoral ministry, family life, cultural analysis, and lessons that can only be learned from hard experience. This book is as much human treasure as spiritual wisdom. It's a read that will both nourish and delight.

Byron Paulus
President, Life Action Ministries

Candid, compelling, insightful, inspiring: Erwin's extraordinary story shows what God's grace and kindness can do through a life fully devoted to Him.

Colin S. Smith
Senior pastor, The Orchard

This is a book about God and His faithfulness in the life of Erwin Lutzer. In it Dr. Lutzer describes how God took him from a remote farm in Canada and providentially directed him, using His people, circumstances and decisions to guide in his life. For thirty five years Pastor Lutzer has consistently modeled servant leadership with humility as senior pastor of The Moody Church. This book will encourage you to trust God in all things and remind you that it is really all about God and His grace.

Bervin Peterson
Chairman, board of elders, The Moody Church

I'm so glad that my friend Erwin Lutzer has written this book to show both the blessings and trials of being a pastor. More than that, this book shows us how God often grows leaders in the most remote circumstances and only in retrospect can we see His remarkable, providential hand. In these pages you will find a ringing affirmation of God's sovereignty in all of our lives, even extending to the details of life.

Dr. Tony Evans
Senior pastor, Oak Cliff Bible Fellowship
President, The Urban Alternative

HE WILL BE THE PREACHER

The Story of God's Providence in My Life

ERWIN W. LUTZER

MOODY PUBLISHERS

CHICAGO

© 2015 by
ERWIN W. LUTZER

Scripture quotations are taken from *The Holy Bible, English Standard Version*® (ESV®), copyright ©2001 by Crossway, a publishing ministry of Good News Publishers. Used by permission. All rights reserved.

Scripture quotations marked KJV are taken from the King James Version.

Edited by Elizabeth Cody Newenhuyse
Interior and cover design: Erik M. Peterson
Cover photograph by Stephen Vosloo. Copyright © 2015 by Moody Publishers.
All rights reserved.

Library of Congress Cataloging-in-Publication Data
Lutzer, Erwin W.
He will be the preacher : the story of God's providence in my life / Erwin W. Lutzer.
    pages cm
Includes bibliographical references.
ISBN 978-0-8024-1306-2
1. Lutzer, Erwin W. 2. Protestant churches--Clergy--Biography. 3. Evangelicalism
—United States. I. Title.
BX4827.L88A3 2015
280'.4092--dc23
[B]
                        2014046546

We hope you enjoy this book from Moody Publishers. Our goal is to provide high-quality, thought-provoking books and products that connect truth to your real needs and challenges. For more information on other books and products written and produced from a biblical perspective, go to www.moodypublishers.com or write to:

Moody Publishers
820 N. LaSalle Boulevard
Chicago, IL 60610

3 5 7 9 10 8 6 4 2

Printed in the United States of America

With affection to the members and friends of The Moody Church whose love and prayers have been an encouragement to me and my family, and whose witness for Christ is proof that the Gospel is still "the power of God unto salvation." Thank you for the privilege of preaching God's Word from this historic pulpit for the past 35 years.

CONTENTS

FOREWORD

I had a difficult time putting down the manuscript of this book as I read it, and I finished it in two sittings. (The interruption was "dinner on the table," so it was really one sitting.) While I was reading, I kept saying to myself, "If I were back teaching seminarians, I would make this book required reading." Why? Because it explains where Christian workers come from and how the Lord calls them, equips them, and enables them to discern His will, carry the burdens, and fight the battles, all to His glory. That's quite an accomplishment for one book, but Dr. Erwin Lutzer has done it, and we are the beneficiaries. It's one of the best ministerial autobiographies I have ever read, and I have read many of them.

This book is much more than an account of one minister's life and ministry. It is the record of how the Lord can work in all His children's lives if only we will let Him. You don't have to be in full-time Christian service to benefit from reading this book. If you major in full-time Christian living, that qualifies you. You not only meet Dr. Lutzer and his wife and watch them mature as parents and servants of the Lord, but you discover that even faithful pastors can have their lives threatened, their churches sued, and their ministries falsely accused.

My wife and I first met Erwin and Rebecca Lutzer when I became pastor of the Moody Church in Chicago in 1971. He was pastoring Edgewater Baptist Church in Chicago and teaching at the Moody Bible Institute. I used to meet with him regularly for prayer, along with Mark Bubeck and Doug Stimers, both of whom were pastoring in the greater Chicago area. We would find a quiet corner in the Moody Memorial Church facilities, share our blessings and burdens, and devote ourselves to praying for God's help in our ministries. Believe me, the Lord heard our prayers and answered them in remarkable ways, some of which are not yet ready for public consumption.

Reading this book is the next best thing to knowing Erwin personally and hearing him preach the Word of God. Any believer in Jesus Christ who takes this book seriously is bound to get a broader view of the challenges involved in church and pastoral ministry today. Ministry is much more than preaching, counseling, marrying, and burying. You will learn from this book how the Lord led Erwin Lutzer to a better understanding of how to deal with globalism, politics, evangelistic outreach, and the many facets of life in the big city. If every pastor and local church would only share in this experience, what a difference it would make in the spread of the gospel!

It's not an easy road, but if the Lord has called us and put us where we are, He will see to it that we will know His will and accomplish it, no matter how impossible it may seem. As Dr. Bob Cook used to say to us in Youth for Christ, "Keep your ministry on a miracle basis. If you can explain what's going on, God didn't do it." Erwin and Rebecca Lutzer have done just that, and so may we.

I pray that the reading of this book leads to the stirring of your heart, the joyful encouragement of your ministry, and a wider vision of your opportunities in today's tangled world.

—WARREN W. WIERSBE

The Improbable Story

On April 3, 1977, I preached my first message from the pulpit of The Moody Church. Standing there on the platform, I said to myself only half seriously, "If they ever call me to be the pastor of this church, I'll say *yes*."

I had not intended to preach at The Moody Church that Sunday morning. After letting my wife, Rebecca, and our two children off at the LaSalle Street door of the church, I began looking for a parking place. Up ahead were cars as far as the eye could see. To my delight, I saw a man cross the street in front of me, get into his car, and drive off. I was gratified that I had a parking place just a hundred feet from the church door.

I found Rebecca in the church lobby, and to my surprise, the pastor, Dr. Warren Wiersbe, walked past me with his coat on.

"Wiersbe, where are you going? It's about ten minutes before the service."

"Erwin Lutzer, I'm sick and I'm on my way home. Will you preach for me this morning?"

And so it was that the very first time Rebecca and I attended a service at The Moody Church, I preached at The Moody Church. That's just one of the many dots God connected in my life, which led me to become the senior pastor of The Moody Church on January 1, 1980—a position I've held for thirty-five years and an honor I'd never envisioned.

Born in a farmhouse five miles from a small town situated on the windswept plains of southern Saskatchewan, Canada, I could never have dreamed that I'd have such a privilege. My early years were filled with milking cows, feeding chickens, and attending a one-room schoolhouse (we got there in a horse-drawn sleigh in winter and a buggy in the summer). As the last-born of five children, I had more time than my siblings to fritter away, often trying to build various gadgets in my father's garage, particularly small wind-driven propellers that I affixed on fence posts.

Yet there was something within me that told me that my destiny didn't lie on the farm. My fascination with Billy Graham in my teen years led me to believe that someday I would be a preacher.

My mother told me that when I was a baby, their pastor who married my parents visited the farmhouse. Before the pastor's wife left, she leaned over the crib, gave me a kiss, and said in German, "He will be the preacher."

Whether this was just an offhand remark or whether this woman was speaking under the inspiration of the Holy Spirit, we'll never know. What we do know is that her prediction came to pass.

DESTINY DECISIONS

The purpose of this book can be simply stated: *It was written to bring glory to God by showing how He led in my life even when I wasn't aware of it.* Ordinary decisions in my life became significant only in retrospect. This is a story of God's providence and faithfulness in response to praying parents. In truth, it is not my story but rather God's story and how I incidentally fit into His plan.

My good friend and fellow pastor Crawford Loritts says that God chooses an assignment for us and then comes and recruits us for the project. I now believe that God came to that farm in Canada and recruited me for the assignment to be a pastor/preacher. Although this was beyond my ability, He would call me to Himself and then equip me for the task.

When driving a car there are many decisions we can make that will not affect our destination. Our speed, whether we stop for lunch or not, whether we're driving with the air conditioner or heater, and many other decisions we make along the way won't affect our destiny. But when the GPS says, "In one mile, make a right turn," we're now faced with a destiny decision that will determine where our journey will end.

Looking back, many of my ordinary decisions turned out to be destiny decisions. We all agree that as we survey our lives, we can see that the providence of God can only be read backwards—only later do we see these decisions as part of a larger, divine plan.

As you read my story, you'll discover how my inexplicable refusal to complete an application for a scholarship in one school led me to another where the direction of my life was forever changed. You'll see how God kept me from a bad marriage even when I was determined to marry someone whom I thought was "my soul mate." Then there's a chance remark by a seminary professor that launched my writing career, and how a providential parking place was a critical step that led me to becoming the pastor of The Moody Church. And through all of this, I'll show how God's faithfulness was with me even in my dark days and sleepless nights.

I am well aware of my limitations, the missed opportunities, and the fact that hundreds of pastors have had a much wider and more impactful ministry than I. Even so, I've written these pages for the encouragement of God's people, and especially for those who think that their future might be limited because of geography or their humble beginnings. And I tell my story to show that the will of God might not be as mysterious as some people think it is; it is revealed in the everyday decisions of life.

A PERSONAL WORD

I apologize to all of my friends and colleagues whose names do not appear in this book. Hundreds of people who have blessed me, and with whom I have worked deserve to have their names in these pages, but I simply couldn't do justice to all of them. So, apart from members of my immediate family and a few notable leaders who've influenced me, very few names are mentioned.

This book is written with deep, heartfelt gratitude for the blessings God has given me. He's given me a lovely, supportive wife, three daughters, and three sons-in-law, all of whom walk with God. He has blessed Rebecca and me with eight delightful grandchildren (nine if you count baby Sarah who is in heaven). None of these blessings are deserved; these are gifts of His gracious mercy. He is the one who has accomplished it all.

A song that's often brought tears to my eyes and is one of my favorites is "God Leads His Dear Children Along." The second and third stanzas are as follows:

Sometimes on the mount where the sun shines so bright,
God leads His dear children along;
Sometimes in the valley, in darkest of night,
God leads His dear children along.

Though sorrows befall us and Satan oppose,
God leads His dear children along;
Through grace we can conquer, defeat all our foes,
God leads His dear children along.

The chorus reads:

Some through the waters, some through the flood,
Some through the fire, but all through the blood;
Some through great sorrow, but God gives a song,
In the night season and all the day long.

And, so it is through mountains and valleys; through dark days and through periods of encouragement and discouragement; when we are affirmed and when we are opposed; when we fail and when we are restored, God leads us. Through the flood, through the fire, but thankfully through the blood.

All glory goes to Jesus Christ who captured my heart when I was fourteen years old and whose gospel I delight to preach.

"Not unto us, O Lord, not unto us
But to thy name be the glory."

Erwin Lutzer
The Moody Church
May 2015

CHAPTER 1

The Farm, Family, and Faith

❧

So who is Billy Graham?" I asked my older sister Esther. She had just come up the stairs in the farmhouse to tell me that we'd be driving to a Youth for Christ rally held in a town about twenty miles from our farm in Saskatchewan, Canada. The attraction was a new feature film being shown in a town hall, and the man she mentioned in connection with it was someone I'd never heard of before: Billy Graham.

"He's an evangelist in the United States," she said, "and thousands of people get saved when he preaches." I knew that the United States was south of Canada, but for all I cared, it could be on some distant planet. The idea of a famous evangelist interested me, but I gave it no further thought. Little did I realize that someday his life would have a great impact on my own.

That night I joined my brothers and sisters to see the film *Mr. Texas,* produced back in the year 1951. I've never forgotten the last scenes of the film when Redd Harper (Mr. Texas) was lying in a hospital bed listening to Billy Graham speaking on *The Hour of Decision.* But even more vivid was the vignette of a youthful Billy Graham preaching to thousands at a stadium crusade. His captivating voice, rapid movements, and sincerity were electrifying. From that day on, I had one earthly hero: Billy Graham.

Perhaps it seems unlikely that a boy of eleven or twelve, born five miles from a town of seventy-five people, would choose Billy Graham as his hero. And it is unlikely, except that this is a story of divine providence, a story of undeserved grace. For as long as I can remember, I had only one serious desire and that was to be a preacher.

Even before I saw the Billy Graham film, I would come home from church, stand in my bedroom, and pretend that I was a pastor preaching a sermon; and for good measure, I led the singing too. So it was quite natural that as a child I would be attracted to the most famous of all preachers—the young evangelist from North Carolina. When I was a teenager, my peers were fans of Elvis; but I chose Billy, listening regularly to *The Hour of Decision* and reading all I could about him. I didn't have the courage to dream that someday I'd meet him, spend twenty minutes with him in my study at The Moody Church, and years later, visit him in his rustic home in North Carolina. But I'm ahead of the story.

Though one of my earliest recollections is preaching in my bedroom, an even earlier memory is playing in the sandbox just outside of the farmhouse. One day I occupied myself with a tin can my mother gave me, using it to try and catch rays of light. I would hold the empty can up to the sun and close the lid as fast as I could; then I took the can to a dark place and opened it, hoping to see a glimmer of light, but alas, no matter how many times I tried, there was only darkness. Later I learned that light, whether physical or spiritual, needs a source—it can't exist on its own.

We had an old Whippet car that had a crank to start the motor.

When it ran, it took us the twenty miles to church during the summer, but snow kept it in the garage all winter. As for the church service, perhaps fifty people attended on a good Sunday, and my most vivid memory was standing on the bench beside my mother during the service. There was singing, a sermon, and friends chatted when it was over. For some reason I disliked going to church, and my father would have to sometimes bribe me with peppermint candies so I'd quit making a fuss and get into the car with everyone else without creating a scene.

One of my Sunday school teachers (who is still living today) told me recently that I was so shy she couldn't get me to speak no matter how hard she tried. When she told us that "Jesus died at Calvary," I assumed she meant "Calgary," a city in the province of Alberta. I remember thinking that we could quite easily drive there and see where Jesus was crucified. My sister Esther later clarified the difference between the two words and assured me that Jesus was not crucified in the neighboring province. At an early age, I wondered why the pastor's sermon wasn't just sent to us in the mail, which would have made going to church unnecessary. Quite obviously I needed some instruction on the larger purpose for attending church and Sunday school.

My father purchased a tractor the year I was born, but we still didn't have a truck. I can remember when all the grain was hauled by horses and a wagon. He had to shovel thousands of bushels of grain, first into a bin during harvest, then at a later date, he shoveled it all back onto a wagon and took it to the grain elevator in a town five miles away. In retrospect, I simply don't know how he did it; the workload was unimaginable.

When a used Ford truck was finally purchased in 1951, the owner brought it to the farm, and my father went into our dingy basement and brought up a wad of money. We watched as he counted out the bills until he reached the agreed-upon price of $1,950. The man said he'd be glad to give Dad a receipt, but Dad said it was unnecessary; they just shook hands and the deal was done. Clearly, those were different days.

Growing up, our collie, Skipper, and I were the best of friends, and he knew when it was time to play "the game." He'd run away and I'd hide among the rows of trees. When Skipper found me, he'd bless me with slobbering licks and kisses. And the moment I said, "Go hide!" there'd be a repeat performance. I always tried to choose a place where I thought he'd never find me, but he always did.

During the Christmas season, our family usually had a Christmas tree and our parents made sure that we always had at least one gift, sometimes two. One year when it was too cold and stormy to go to town, my mother took a barren tree branch and used it as a Christmas tree. I remember getting a toy truck that looked rather familiar: it was the truck my brother was given when he was younger, but it had been given a fresh coat of green paint. Another year our mother—God bless her—wrapped a twenty-five-cent piece for each of us as an extra gift.

As the last-born of five children, I had definite advantages. For one thing, I had extra time on my hands since the chores were usually done by my two older brothers. For another, my parents had relaxed some of their discipline, so my sister Esther complained that I got away with things she'd been disciplined for—and I'm sure she was right. Our parents were still very strict: no sports on Sunday, no television (even if it had been available, which it wasn't), and, for the most part, no social events at school. Movies were deemed to be sub-moral, and such things as attending a school dance were clearly off-limits.

But boys will be boys.

THE FOOLISHNESS OF A FARM BOY

It's a miracle that most boys actually survive life on the farm, given the opportunities to do foolish and often risky things, such as driving a tractor recklessly into a ditch, or crawling through a culvert installed under a road to drain water from one side to the other where I'd inch my way through this narrow, corrugated steel tunnel, just barely wide enough for my shoulders. If I'd have gotten stuck halfway through, or had become claustrophobic, or panicked, no help would have been available since the culvert was about a half mile from the farmyard. Only Skipper knew where I was.

One day my sister Esther and I were chasing a stray cat in the hayloft of the barn when I fell through a hole used for a pulley. I landed on a six-inch-square beam and was knocked unconscious. My father and brother carried me into the house where I woke up about an hour later not knowing what had happened and seeing my mother across the room busy at her sewing machine. They told me that I mumbled incoherently after the fall, and that I couldn't walk, so they carried me and laid me on the couch with the hope that I'd recover. For weeks after this concussion, I could only walk slowly; to run would cause my head to explode with pain. In retrospect, I think of the permanent damage that could have been done and how, in today's world, we'd rush a child in that condition to a doctor. Back then, however, doctors were thought of as a last resort; if injured you were expected to recover on your own.

When I broke my arm falling off a neighbor's horse, I tried to hide it from my parents by enduring the pain and just using my right hand, not my left. As expected, my mother noticed it within a matter of minutes. This time I was taken to the doctor and had my arm strapped to my chest for several weeks. Perhaps that is why, to this day, my left arm is shorter than my right.

Of course, while living on a farm, temptation, as we generally think of it, was minimal. There was quite literally no convenient way to get into trouble. Yes, we were disciplined for failure to follow orders: feeding the chickens, milking the cows, or bringing wood to the house were duties that were to be gladly performed. Some boys would sneak a smoke at school, but for the Lutzer children, such temptations were easily resisted. We had been taught that God hated sin and that if we participated in it, the consequences would come back to haunt us.

SCHOOL DAZE

During my grades one to three, we went to a one-room schoolhouse three miles away, traveling with the horse and buggy during the summer and the sleigh during the winter. We had a predictable pattern: when we got out of bed, our breakfast was waiting; following that, a passage was read from the German Bible and we prayed as a family. Then our dad would ready the horse, and off we would go to school. My older brothers and sisters took the responsibility for the details of getting to and from school, so I had few worries.

I learned early on that children could indeed be cruel, hurting others with angry words and callous behavior. One of my greatest heartaches to this day is the hostility the children of one family showed toward us and a third family (yes, there were only three families of children that attended this school). One family had three hate-filled children who made school life difficult for us all. Filled with resentment and jealousy, these three children—I would call them *evil*—would taunt us and especially the other family, whom they clearly hated. We Lutzer children were caught in the middle, often watching and listening in silence as these abusive children berated the others by calling them names and ridiculing everything they did and said.

Even as I write these words, I wish we could relive those days and side with the children of the third family who were so cruelly treated. We Lutzer children should have had the courage to let those hostile kids know that we wouldn't tolerate their abuse of us or others.

I recall one of those boys speaking kindly to a stray dog, and when the dog came close, tempted by something to eat, the boy kicked the animal as hard as he could, sending the dog yelping into the distance. A few days later, the same dog trusted this boy again, and the same thing happened. I realize that all of us have a sin nature, and that children struggle with anger, resentment, and jealousy. But there are some children who seem to be born with a special bent toward cruelty and evil.

Although most of the Lutzer children were compliant toward our parents, our brother Albert was a typical strong-willed firstborn. But he turned out to be a hero one winter day when coats that were hung too close to the hot furnace started a fire in the basement of the schoolhouse. Since the school didn't have a phone, Albert put some of the schoolgirls on a sleigh, threw a blanket over them (it was midwinter), and made the horse run as fast as possible to the closest neighbor. Since most of the farmers had phones, word spread quickly, and many of them came and shoveled snow into the building to keep it from burning to the ground.

The other fire I clearly remember began when Albert stepped on a chair and poked his head through the open space of an enclosed closet whose walls didn't reach all the way up to the ceiling. He suspected that there were cleaning supplies in the closet, which he thought he needed to sweep the floor, a chore the teacher had assigned to him. In order to see behind the boards, he stood on a chair, then cocked his head and peered through the eighteen-inch opening above the boards while holding a burning roll of paper to light the darkness. When cinders fell onto a mop, it started to burn, so he had to rip several of the boards off to get inside the enclosure; thankfully, the flames were quickly extinguished.

The explanation he gave to the teacher was that he had pushed another student against the closet, breaking the boards; then he repaired the damage as best he could. Surely, the teacher knew better, but she said little.

Thankfully, at the end of my third grade, the school was closed for lack of students. For my fourth grade, we switched to another school in the area with an entirely different leadership and atmosphere. This school was about four miles in the opposite direction from our farm.

The change was well worth it; here there were no hateful families bent on deriding others (the teacher, Mrs. Watson, would never have tolerated such behavior). By then, Albert and my sister Ruth had finished grade school, but Harold and Esther still attended, so the three of us continued our education together. Horse and sleigh in winter; horse and buggy in spring and fall.

THE ONE-ROOM SCHOOLHOUSE

If the one-room schoolhouse had drawbacks educationally, it made up for it in the richness of relationships. The teacher would begin with the row of first-graders (perhaps five or six students), explain the subject matter, and then give them an assignment. Then she would go to the next row with the second-graders and repeat the process, helping them to get started on their work for the day. Our one-room schoolhouse had all eight grades, though sometimes one grade had only two or three pupils (one or two grades might not have any students at all). Only years later did I realize that students in city schools had a separate room for each grade! "What a breeze for the teacher!" I thought.

Of course, the older students constantly challenged the teacher, testing them to see where the limits actually were. Could we write notes to one another in class? Yes, as long as we weren't caught. Could someone go to the restroom without permission? Yes, but if you stayed too long someone might be sent to get you. Could you talk sassy to the teacher? No, not unless you wanted to stay after school or be spanked (or your parents would be talked to).

In the fifth grade, we had a new teacher, Mrs. Barmby, who was newly widowed and living in a house adjacent to the schoolhouse. She was tenderhearted, cried easily, and we often took advantage of her sensitivity and kindness.

Embedded in my memory is this incident:

"Who took the dustpan and left it outside, behind the school?"

Mrs. Barmby was livid. When she became angry, her face not only turned red, but her lips quivered. Now, standing in front of the class with a ruler in her hand, she waited patiently for an answer to her question.

Dead silence.

"Since the person who did it refuses to admit it, I want all of you to line up here for a spanking!" By now she was hollering.

I spoke up. "I'll say I did it, but I didn't!"

It's not that I was particularly brave. But I reasoned that it was foolish for the whole class to get a spanking, if one person could "take the hit" for the other dozen or so students.

Mrs. Barmby rejected my suggestion. "I don't want to spank you; I want to spank the one who did it!" The pitch of her voice was up another decibel.

Just then, her own son George, who lived with her next to the school, sauntered into the room, ten minutes late, as was his habit.

"George, did *you* carry the dustpan to the back of the school?" Her voice was more subdued.

"Yes."

George held out his hand and was slapped with the ruler by his own mother in the presence of us all. We had just averted a minor disaster.

Mrs. Barmby, bless her, did not lose her temper often and became teary-eyed when she talked to us about her experiences of pain and sorrow as a widow. As teachers go, she was reasonable and kind. Because her angry outbursts were few, we often became rowdy and lax, and she was far too tolerant of us.

Many years later, long after we moved to Chicago, my wife, Rebecca, and I stopped by her home on one of our visits to Canada, and I was able to share the gospel with her. She said that what she remembered about me was that when she began teaching evolution, I raised my hand and objected, saying that I believed God created everything. Apparently my interest in apologetics (defending the faith) began early in life. She died several years ago, and I truly hope that her faith was in Christ.

In this school, whether it was Mrs. Watson or Mrs. Barmby, we knew that we were expected to be kind, play fair, and use our recess for better things than berating one another. And yet, I felt a great deal of pain in those early years. Because I was not athletic, I often felt as though I were a second-class student who stayed out of trouble but was not fully accepted by the other students. When the students divided into teams to play softball, I was usually among the last chosen. I was glad when I passed into the ninth grade, for then life in the old country schoolhouse was over.

"HE WILL BE THE PREACHER"

All five of us were born in the house our parents were living in at the time of our births. I have often been deeply moved by an account given by the midwife who was on hand for our births. She was one of Mother's friends and though she had no training, she played the role of a midwife. She remembered specifically that almost immediately after I was born, she and my father (and possibly my mother got out of bed to join them), held me and knelt to dedicate me to God (perhaps they did the same when my brothers and sisters were born, but if so, the midwife never mentioned it). Mother also told me that when the pastor of the church who married them visited, the pastor's wife bent over and gave me a kiss while I was sleeping in the crib and said in German, *"Er wird der Prediger sein"* (he will be the preacher).

As I recall these incidents, they reinforce my belief that God called me even back then to be a preacher and to have the opportunity to share God's Word with many people. The God who so graciously guided my parents, even when they were unaware of it, has guided the footsteps of their five children. We were all profoundly shaped by their prayers and the example they set for us.

But parents cannot convert a child. It is not enough for a child to be encouraged to pray a prayer that might or might not result in salvation. Parents should not try to "get the chicken out of the egg," so to speak. They can explain the gospel, they can and should pray for their child, but ultimately, conversion is God's business.

AM I SAVED?

Obviously, growing up in a home where the gospel was front and center, I learned early on that I had to accept Christ as my personal Savior or be lost forever. As a child, I would often pray that Jesus would come into my heart, but I felt no different after the prayer. So I assumed that I wasn't saved, and even went so far as to think that I couldn't be saved. Bizarre as this now seems, I remember thinking to myself that I should read the book of Revelation to see if I was mentioned there as someone who was an apostate, unable to be converted.

We also attended evangelistic services where the gospel was preached and a long "altar call" followed. At the end of the service, the congregation would sing an invitation song (almost always "Just As I Am"), and then those who wanted to be saved were to come to the front to receive Christ as Savior. But I was so shy, I remember thinking to myself, "If I have to go forward in the presence of all these people to be saved, I guess I will just have to go to hell."

In retrospect, I'm surprised by how aware I was that I was a sinner who needed to be forgiven. At about the age of fourteen, while I was standing in our small farmhouse kitchen drinking water from a common family dipper, my mother said, "Dad and I think it's time for you to get saved." I remember my exact words: "I've tried to get saved, but it doesn't work for me." They explained that Christ had to be received by faith, whether I felt changed or not afterwards. The three of us knelt together in the living room of the old farmhouse, and there I brought my doubting heart to the Lord and prayed to accept Him as mine.

The next day I knew I had been converted. I remember walking into the garage on the farm and thinking to myself, "I know that I know God . . ." In fact, His presence was so real I thought I should be capable of anything. The doubts were gone; I knew that from now on I would never have to pray to receive Christ again—this time "it worked," and my life would be different because of it.

Today, I marvel at my parents' perception. What made them think it was time for me to accept Christ as my Savior? Did they notice that I was under conviction of sin? Did they see that my casual and perhaps hostile attitude toward family devotions demonstrated that I wasn't saved? I never did ask them these questions, but I thank God they initiated the discussion.

As I grew and studied theology, I've often reflected back to this time and wondered when I really was converted. Was it during those early days when I prayed on my own that Jesus would come into my heart but I had no assurance that He accepted me, or was I converted at the time I remember the clearest—when I prayed with my parents to accept Christ by faith? Although many people have been converted by "accepting Jesus into their hearts," I have concluded that this is not the best way to communicate the gospel.

Since that time I've helped many people understand that if we believe that when Jesus died on the cross and rose again—if we believe that He did all that ever will be necessary for us to come into God's presence—and if we embrace that for ourselves, we will not only be saved but know it. In other words, salvation involves accepting the finished work of Christ on our behalf.

Regardless of whether or not I had previously been saved, by the age of fourteen I now had the assurance that I was converted—and I've never doubted it since. There's always been this deep settled peace that God was my Father and that I was one of His children. One thing is certain, each child must have their own faith; the faith of their parents cannot save them. And unless their parents' faith is claimed for themselves, it will wash away when the temptations of life lure them in the direction of the world.

There were times—and I don't remember how old I was—when I would run out in the fields at night and look up at the stars and pray. I was literally mesmerized by the immensity of God. Once, during such a time of worship, God gave me a revelation of the sinfulness of my heart. I realized then, that if He were to send me to hell, He would be righteous in doing so, but I begged for His mercy that I wouldn't be condemned.

The God who saved me would now lead me in ways that no one could have predicted. The trek from a small Canadian farm to being the pastor of one of America's best-known churches is one that is marked by divine providence.

Fifty years later, I visited the old farmhouse and knelt in the same living room where I had been converted to give thanks to God for all that He had done in my life since those childhood days.

"I thank him who has given me strength, Christ Jesus our Lord, because he judged me faithful, appointing me to his service... To the King of the ages, immortal, invisible, the only God, be honor and glory forever and ever. Amen" (1 Timothy 1:12, 17).

And Amen.

CHAPTER 2

Shaped by Praying Parents

W hen he was in his forties and fifties, my father often suffered
from what we now believe were panic attacks. He would tell
us that he was dying, thinking he would soon have a heart attack, or
that he had cancer or some other ailment. Our oldest brother Albert
would rush him to the hospital, and we children expected him to die
at any moment. In fact, one spring he even predicted he would not live
to help with the harvest in the fall.

Our father, in a state of worry and thinking he might die at any moment, even checked himself into a mental facility. While there, he was
visited by a psychiatrist who tried to find the source of his depression
and fears, but there were no clear answers. Before he was released, he
was given some medication that did help him sleep better.

One day he called all five of us to his bedside to tell us that he was
dying. "Take good care of Mother," he said, and "we will meet again
in heaven." As a boy of about ten or eleven, I remember crying uncon-
trollably, thinking to myself that I would never be happy again. To lose

my father was unthinkable. me too

After a battery of tests at the hospital, the doctor told Albert, "There is nothing wrong with your dad; he will live to be a hundred." Actually, the doctor missed it by six years. My dad lived to be 106! And a few years after his death, my mother died at 103. They were married for seventy-seven years, and as I have often said, my parents lived so long that I'm sure until our dad died, all of their friends in heaven thought, "The Lutzers just didn't make it!"

But the Lutzers did make it to heaven! Of that we can be sure!

As Gustav's and Wanda's children, we heard very little of their incredible childhood. They had lived through dark days but chose to put their past behind them. On occasion, to correct our complaining, they would remind us that we didn't know how good we had it; then they would share an incident from their past to show what life was like when they were our age. Even though we felt rebuked, we couldn't relate to the hardships they had endured.

If childhood trauma is often the cause of panic attacks, it is not difficult to understand my father's depression and fears. Suffering made our parents who they were; suffering helped them understand the nature of sin and the great need we all have for redemption. And they were both introduced to acute suffering at a very young age.

GERMANS IN THE UKRAINE

At the end of the nineteenth century, many German families migrated to the Ukraine thanks to what appeared to be a generous offer from the Russian government. But for many Germans, living in the Ukraine was indeed a test of loyalties. On the one hand, they rendered allegiance to Russia, their adopted homeland; on the other hand, they were of German origin and still keenly interested in the revival of the German nation and the rule of Kaiser Wilhelm I who intended to usher in the "Second Reich" (*Reich* meaning *empire*) under Germany's leadership.

My father, Gustav, born in 1902, was the fourth of nine children. Summer months were busy with planting and caring for the fields, but in the winter when there was less work, he was permitted to attend school. At a young age, Gustav was frequently in charge of his younger siblings while his sister worked in the fields. About the age of seven, he was sent away from home to work herding cattle at the home of his half-sister, Amelia, and her husband. Children were looked upon as a necessity for the survival of the family, and child labor was customary and acceptable. These relatives were not kind to the young Gustav.

One day when Gustav was sitting on a rocker, he awoke with a jolt, then, somewhat unthinkingly, grabbed the pot of potatoes from the stove and dumped them into a wooden container. Enraged, his half-sister grabbed an iron poker from the stove and hit him on the head so severely that blood squirted onto the wall. Subdued by what she'd done, she worked to arrest the hemorrhage by packing the wound with bread crumbs. Gustav was promised a pair of boots if he didn't tell his mother. At Christmas when his mother came to visit, he kept his promise, but when his mother patted his head, she found the wound under his thick dark hair. This incident prompted her to take Gustav home until summer was over. In the fall, the needs of the family were so great that he was again sent away to work with another family to help earn a living.

The Lutzers were Lutheran, attending church whenever possible. The Bible was read in the home, prayers were offered, and a respect for God was both modeled and expected. My dad remembered his mother kneeling in church and praying with a shawl covering her head. Though the family was religious, the doctrine of salvation by faith was not clearly taught.

REFUGEES IN AFGHANISTAN

After the outbreak of World War I in 1914, Russia decreed that all Germans in the Ukraine would have to be deported lest they become spies for Germany, or in some way, side with Germany in the war. Gustav's family joined the others on a journey that would lead to hardship, sorrow, and for many family members, death.

The Lutzer family began their uncertain journey with a ten-day trip moving along a river, living on a barge that had a lower deck where the people could sleep. After that, they traveled with horses and wagons for three weeks, shuffling from one village to another. The Russian government demanded that the villagers feed the refugees then move them on to the next village where the process started all over again. The Lutzers and other refugees were eventually loaded into freight train cars to continue their journey. These were cattle cars without toilet facilities and with only a few openings high on the sides. Large shelves had been built, so that each boxcar could carry forty people stacked in three layers. When the trains stopped, people ran out with kettles to avail themselves of the hot water that was put out for them. Sometimes the trains started off without warning, separating parents from children forever. The distress among the refugees can only be imagined as they journeyed into the unknown.

The Lutzers continued south, on to Kabul, the capital of Afghanistan, which was already occupied by the Russian military. My dad remembered leaving the barracks with his mother to try to find some milk for the sick siblings, but they returned empty-handed. Illness spread throughout the camps. The hot weather, combined with severe malnutrition, resulted in many deaths. His seven-year-old brother and five-year-old sister died on the same day. The next day, his nine-year-old sister died. They were buried in a mass grave with other children.

Most heartbreaking was the death of his mother, who at the age of forty-two died of typhoid fever two years after they arrived in Afghanistan. She had been admitted to the hospital where the children were not permitted to visit her. She had no opportunity to give any last words to her family, and the children received few, if any, reports of her condition, until they were informed of her death.

Fourteen-year-old Gustav, already in grief over the death of his brother and two sisters, now looked at the form of his dead mother in the wooden coffin and refused to be comforted. There was no funeral service, just the lowering of the plain coffin into the ground next to the corpse of another woman—all in the presence of the grieving family. Overcome with grief, Gustav lay on the ground and sobbed. His father tried to comfort the family while coping with his own grief as best he could. For two more years, the family lived in crowded conditions shared with others.

In late 1918, when the war ended, the Lutzers were permitted to return to their homestead in the Ukraine. The family worked hard to get reestablished. Gustav's father, Wilhelm, weakened by the horrors of war, took ill in 1926, and so he began to read the Bible to prepare for his death. He admonished young Gustav, "Don't live a worldly life, don't smoke, but trust in the Lord." My dad never forgot those words because they were said only to him, not to the other children. Shortly after, Wilhelm went to his eternal rest.

The year following his father's death, my dad, remembering his father's words, began attending the Church of God. There he met a young Christian woman from another village. He loved her and soon a wedding was planned, but her parents did not think that Gustav was worthy of their daughter, so the wedding was called off. Heartbroken, Gustav accepted his loss, and he continued to attend church and was later converted. Meanwhile, God had someone else prepared for

Gustav, and to meet her he would have to emigrate to Canada.

At the age of twenty-five, hoping for the opportunity to have a better life, Gustav said goodbye to the family members with whom he had lived through great sorrow and hardship. By train, and later by ship, he sailed to Liverpool, England. From there he boarded the *Empress of Scotland* and sailed to Canada. He met the relative who agreed to support him, and began working on a farm. My dad was glad that there was a seat on the plow pulled by horses. In the Ukraine, he had always walked behind the horses while plowing; now he could sit and be pulled along with the plow. "When I saw there was a seat on the plow, I determined that I would never return to the Ukraine to live again."

WANDA'S STORY

Wanda Ludtke was the third of nine children, also born into a German family in the Ukraine (about two hundred miles from where her future husband, Gustav, was born). Wanda's father, Julius, had a heart for God. He read his Bible faithfully and listened to the sermons given by the pastors. He warned his children about the consequences of sin, and stressed the need for repentance and living a holy life. The family was Lutheran, attended church whenever possible, and said prayers each evening before bedtime.

Incredibly, in 1913, one year before World War I began, Wanda's father had sailed to the United States and found work in Chicago, with the intention of bringing his entire family over at a later date. He wrote home telling about how good life was in the United States compared to the Ukraine. The women "just have to open their window and bread and milk is delivered to their house!" Of the big buildings in Chicago, he wrote, "Only God could have made them! They are too huge for man to have built!" I've often thought that he could never have dreamed that one day one of his grandsons would be the pastor of a church in this big city.

But with the outbreak of World War I, Julius was able to book a ticket on the very last available passenger ship that left the United States for the Ukraine. From then on, ordinary citizens were not allowed to travel on the ships as all the vessels were mobilized to transport soldiers and war supplies. God in His mercy allowed him to return to his family just in time to help them through the horrors of war.

In the summer of 1915, the Ludtke family was ordered to leave for Siberia. They had only one horse to pull the loaded wagon as they began their journey that would be filled with hardship, sorrow, and for some, death. Day after day they traveled, children with their parents, trudging alongside of the wagon. En route, many families slept outside, in barns, or in straw piles with pigs surrounding them. The villagers were asked to give them food, but at times they had nothing to share with the hordes of refugees. The family chewed on dried bread that they had brought along with them.

Part of the journey to the Ukraine involved crossing a river on a barge. My mother remembered a woman sitting near the edge of the barge heating a pot of water on an open fire. Her little daughter ran toward her and accidentally fell overboard. The distraught mother could only watch as her precious child bobbed in the water and eventually disappeared beneath the waves. Rescue was impossible. Such were the hardships and dangers facing the refugees.

Once across the river, they were transported to the train station in wagons that had been arranged for them by the government. Just like Gustav's family, people were herded into freight cars like cattle. And due to the lack of toilet facilities, many became sick. The few who had food, clutched it, keeping it for themselves or their children. In these deplorable conditions, Wanda's mother gave birth to a baby.

LIFE IN SIBERIA

At last they arrived in Siberia. There were, of course, thousands of people who needed housing and food, but the government took no responsibility for feeding them. Death entered these cramped quarters. Most heartbreaking for Wanda was the death of Lydia, her six-year-old sister who was two years younger than herself. The two had become close friends, playing and talking together, but now Lydia was dead. Their mother clothed her precious daughter in a dress that she made from her own white underskirt. To their dismay, Lydia's body had to lie on the porch for a whole week waiting to be buried because the Communist revolution was in full swing and heavy street fighting erupted.

When there was a lull in the fighting, Wanda's father, Julius, with the help of a young man, placed his daughter's body in a rough wooden coffin that he built, and buried her in a grave with another child. Neither her mother nor any of her siblings were present as Lydia was lowered into the ground. When their mother heard that her child was buried with another, she became troubled. To ease his wife's grief, Julius found a plot, and as best he could, dug a shallow hole so Lydia could be buried in her own grave. The family felt the loss keenly, but perhaps no one grieved more deeply than Wanda.

In November of 1918, the war ended, and with it came the defeat of Germany. Now the Ludtke family was free to return to the Ukraine. They joined a large group of refugees, and shortly after their departure, the Communists closed the borders and didn't allow refugees to return to the Ukraine. Once again the providence of God guided them.

At the age of fifteen, Wanda had to work for a farmer, hoeing sugar beets, potatoes, and other vegetables. There were barns to clean and manure to spread. In the winter, she learned to operate a spinning wheel, using flax to make thread for mending sacks. The rest of the children also worked, doing the best they could to help the family. But they never forgot what their father had said about life in the United States: the American women had bread and milk brought to their houses! Their father, Julius, recalling his year in Chicago, encouraged his two unmarried daughters to emigrate to the big city.

Wanda, now twenty, and her older sister, Martha, twenty-two, were willing to take the risk and travel to the United States, but because of restrictive immigration policies they went to Canada instead. Saying goodbye was very difficult since the sisters had hardly ever been away from their parents. Later, the young women would learn that their mother spent three days in bed mourning their departure, knowing that almost certainly she would never see them again.

So it was, they arrived in Saskatchewan, Canada, and found themselves working for two different farm families who had requested immigrant help. Wanda liked it when she was asked to hoe the garden, because then in her loneliness, she could cry all she liked and no one could see her.

She was invited by a distant relative to transfer to a different farm near the town of Lang, Saskatchewan. She disliked her new environment; here, among other things, she had to resist the unwanted advances of a hired man. But a friend encouraged her to stay, so she thought she'd endure the situation for just a few months. And humanly speaking, *the destiny of all of us children would be determined by her proximity to a small church just a half mile away.*

Although baptized a Lutheran, my mother knew she had never been born again. She was delighted to learn that there were special meetings in the small church in the town of Lang, and that the services were in German! After some powerful preaching, when the invitation was given for people to come forward and pray, Wanda responded immediately and accepted Christ as Savior. However, she didn't have the assurance she desired. The next night as the congregation sang, "Have you been to Jesus for the cleansing power? Are you washed in the blood of the Lamb?" she again made her way to the altar. That evening she had an overwhelming sense of assurance of salvation; she said later it was as though she experienced the glory of God and entered the Holy of Holies. From then on, she never doubted that she belonged to God.

LET ME WALK YOU HOME

One day, on her knees in the church during the prayer time, Wanda heard an unfamiliar voice praying with such sincerity that she knew the young man walked with God. She looked up in an attempt to get a glimpse of him since she hadn't yet met him.

Wanda was both pleased and surprised when a few weeks later, following a church service, this young man asked if he could walk her home. Together they walked out of the town, passing an old graveyard as they made their way to the farm. By the time they arrived at her house, Gustav Lutzer asked Wanda if she would marry him. In my dad's words, "She didn't say yes and she didn't say no." Wanda told him that she would have to think about it. It did not take her long to decide, and a few days later when he repeated his proposal, she responded with a *yes*.

Three weeks after that walk to her home, on July 25, 1931, they were married in the small-town church. They had intended for it to be a small wedding, but the entire congregation wanted to be part of this—the first wedding in the church. Following the ceremony, the bride and groom traveled by horse and buggy to a farm just on the other side of the town for the reception. The church people prepared what little they had during the height of the Depression, and everyone enjoyed a lovely dinner. Some people gave the young couple what they could spare from their household items: a plate, a bowl, a serving spoon. One Lutheran woman gave some pillowcases, and the church gave them a quilt. The pastor gave a message that was followed by singing and testimonies of God's goodness. People remarked that it was one of the most wonderful weddings they had ever attended.

So it was that this marriage that began after an extremely short courtship lasted for seventy-seven years.

A HOME WHERE GOD WAS FIRST

From the beginning, Gustav and Wanda gave God first place in their marriage. Every single day after breakfast we had a reading from the German Bible, followed by prayer, almost always on our knees. As they grew in their love for each other, they also grew in their love for God. It was this personal relationship with God that carried them through difficult days.

I remember one particularly difficult season when hail destroyed our crops in a matter of minutes, and there was still a mortgage on our land that needed to be paid. My parents asked us all to get on our knees to thank God for His goodness. They assured us that we would make it; we had chickens that laid eggs and cows that gave us milk—we would manage somehow. And manage we did.

How my parents prayed! With earnestness and consistency, they prayed that we would be kept from sin, and that we would love righteousness and hate iniquity. They prayed that "our sin would find us out," and that we would come to know Christ as Savior. They taught us to be generous and to acknowledge God in all of our ways.

During the times when my father had panic attacks, he apparently lacked assurance of salvation. Sometimes he would bring the milk into the house after evening chores and then go back to the barn to pray.

There were times when he prayed so loudly we could hear him all the way to the farmhouse. Later, as he became more knowledgeable of the Scriptures, he came to the "full assurance of faith." And, by the way, he suffered no more panic attacks after the age of sixty.

In their later years, after moving from the farm to the city of Regina, they did much entertaining. They would invite missionaries, traveling evangelists, widows, and any lonely friends into their home. As one evangelist put it, "It was impossible to eat at the Lutzers' without the conversation drifting to spiritual things . . . they wanted to talk about Jesus."

On one occasion, they invited a miracle-working, self-proclaimed apostle to their house for lunch. While there, he made this prophecy: "Wanda, something dreadful is going to happen to you within the next few days." This, of course, made her fearful; she could not shake the anxiety of what might come to pass. When she realized that this "prophecy" was from the Devil and not God, she broke the fearful spell by singing, "There is power in the blood." As you might guess, nothing dreadful happened, further proving that this was a false prophet.

LONG LIVES AND PRAYERFUL HEARTS

Back in 1976, Dad was told he had cancer, so we had a forty-fifth wedding celebration for my parents because we didn't think my dad would live until their fiftieth. But when the elders of the church prayed for him, the cancer disappeared; we were able to have a fiftieth anniversary, then a sixtieth, then a sixty-fifth, and finally a seventieth. After that, they wanted no more celebrations, even though they were still married for seven more years—a total of seventy-seven, to be exact.

At their seventieth anniversary, I was sitting beside my mother and asked, "Mother, do you know the names of all of your great-grandchildren?" (there were about twenty-five at the time). She dismissed my comment with a wave of her hand. "Oh yes, I have a prayer list and I mention each one to our heavenly Father every day!" When she died, we found her prayer list with 121 names: all of her children, grandchildren, and great-grandchildren, along with missionaries and friends. Yes, she knew how to pray!

When Dad was one hundred years old, at my wife Rebecca's suggestion, I knelt beside him as he was reading his Bible and asked if he would give me a blessing just like the patriarchs blessed their sons so many centuries ago. Dad laid his hands on my head and prayed a prayer that I'm sure made heaven take notice.

A word to the reader: if you have a Christian father who is still living, ask him for a "blessing." Don't wait until he's a hundred, or it might not happen.

THE LEGACY CONTINUES

When my sister Ruth and her husband, Richard, became missionaries to Mexico with Wycliffe Bible Translators in the early 1960s, my father said to his new son-in-law, "We always wanted to share the gospel with people, but couldn't do that very well because of the language barrier [however, they eventually learned to both read and speak English], and so we pray that our children would be able to share the gospel with many." Ruth and Richard fulfilled my parents' wish and shared the gospel with many in Mexico.

My sister Esther was a missionary in Gabon, Africa, for thirty years, going from village to village doing medical work and sharing the gospel. Only heaven knows how many came to Christ because of her consistent witness.

My brother Harold and his wife, Charlene, were, for many years, the directors of a revival center in Regina, Saskatchewan, working with revival teams and encouraging a much-needed spiritual awakening in Canada. Their six children are walking with God and continue to perpetuate our parents' legacy.

Our oldest brother Albert and his wife, Jean, experienced a great tragedy when their oldest child, Dallas, was killed in a car accident at the age of sixteen. He and another teenager were in the backseat of a car on their way to a Bible quiz when their car hit black ice and skidded into the path of an oncoming truck. A young mother, who was captain of the quiz team, sitting in the front seat, and the two teens in the back were killed instantly; only the driver survived unhurt.

God used this tragedy to motivate Albert and Jean to donate land for what today is the largest ranch camp in Canada, where more than two thousand teenagers come each summer to be taught the Bible, and enjoy swimming, hiking, and above all, horseback riding. The Dallas Valley Ranch Camp has introduced hundreds, if not thousands, of children to faith in Jesus Christ.

The five children of Gustav and Wanda have shared the gospel either directly or indirectly with tens of thousands of people. Even to this day our parents' prayers are being answered.

FINAL WORDS

At the age of 105, my father was sitting in a wheelchair with his eyes closed as Rebecca and I were talking with my mother. At his age, my father would often begin a sentence but not have the words to complete it. This time, he looked up suddenly and spoke a complete sentence in German without the slightest hesitation. Translated, he said, "We have been speaking about the present, but now it is time to speak about eternity and the glory of God." That was one of the last complete sentences he spoke before he died several months later.

Before my mother died, she had told my sister Esther, who was helping care for her in a nursing home, "When I die, I don't want you to cry but to shout 'hallelujah'!"

A few moments after the New Year began in January 2012, it was clear that mother was about to breathe her last breath. Just then, a caregiver named Rachel entered the room. Esther, now dissolving in tears, was hardly in a condition to shout, "Hallelujah!" But Rachel, standing beside Mother's bed, raised her hands and prayed a beautiful prayer giving praise to God, then said, "Hallelujah, Wanda has gone to be with the Lord!"

Rachel actually worked on another floor but was assigned to my mother's floor that evening to fill in for an aide who was ill. What's more, though Esther had met Rachel that evening, she (Esther) didn't know that Rachel was a Christian. And, furthermore, Rachel knew nothing of Mother's request! Since Esther couldn't fulfill my mother's request to shout 'hallelujah,' God brought the right caregiver onto Mother's floor on the right evening so that her last prayer would be answered!

Our lives were shaped by these simple, imperfect, but godly parents who prayed us into the kingdom and prayed that we would serve the Lord. I personally attribute my calling to preach the gospel to the prayers of my parents. They didn't allow their hardships to destroy them but rather to motivate them to pursue God with all their hearts. If they could speak today, they would tell us to pray for our children even as they prayed for us!

The righteous flourish like the palm tree . . .
They still bear fruit in old age;
They are ever full of sap and green,
To declare that the LORD is upright; he is my Rock.
—*Psalm 92:12, 14–15*

CHAPTER 3

God Leads His Dear Children Along

❧

If I was going to be a preacher, I had to break out of my shyness. My sisters will verify that when we had company on the farm, I would sometimes try to hide; in fact, on at least one occasion I hid under the bed until one of them came and encouraged me to come out of hiding, and helped by pulling me out of my hiding place. When a neighbor who often teased me would come for a visit, I would run into the wheat field until he left.

But now I was fourteen, and the country school I attended only went to eighth grade. Since there were no high schools in our area, the decision was made that I would take ninth grade by correspondence. I was supposed to read the textbooks, do the assignments, then send them in to be graded each week. There were twenty lessons per semester. By nature, I like to do things quickly and thought that studying the textbooks before doing the lessons was simply too much trouble. However, I remember sketching pictures of Billy Graham in the margins of my books. So, I bungled my way through, and in the end, I passed my ninth grade, but just barely.

In my early teens I struggled with anger. I especially felt anger toward my strict parents, anger toward the work of the farm, and anger with my sheltered life. In retrospect, I really had nothing to be angry about, but at the time I thought I did. On a few occasions I had serious meltdowns and lashed out, primarily in the seclusion of my bedroom. But there were weeks on end that I gave my parents the silent treatment, talking to them only about the necessary issues of what needed to be done on the farm. I knew I was hurting them. The only redeeming factor was that after I left for boarding school and gained a sense of my own independence, I had a very warm relationship with them. As I gained maturity, I came to realize I had the best parents any child could ask for. And of course, as the years progressed, we grew closer and closer in our fellowship, mutual love, and respect.

Like every teenager, I had to leave home to be introduced to the real world.

HIGH SCHOOL, HERE I COME

For tenth grade, I went to a Christian boarding school about a hundred miles from our farm. Briercrest was a campus that housed both a Bible school and a high school. Since my siblings attended school there, it was only natural that I would follow in their footsteps, and so in the fall of 1956, I enrolled in the tenth grade. The days of "correspondence" were over, and now I was in the classroom with dozens of other students.

This was the first of many experiences of loneliness. I spent time daydreaming of home and life on the farm. Of course, I made friends quite quickly, and soon I loved my roommates, my studies, and my school. But relating to my peers was not always easy for this shy farm boy.

I might fail!

This high school posted our exam grades in alphabetical order on a bulletin board. After the midterm exams in the tenth grade, I remember how embarrassed I was when I got an F in both geometry and algebra. While other students touted their impressive grades, I felt very much humiliated by my poor performance. Perhaps—and I am looking for an excuse here—it was because I learned very little the previous year when I took the ninth grade by correspondence. Years later when a classmate of mine heard me preach, she said to a friend, "Just to think I knew him when he was failing tenth grade!" Thankfully, as the year progressed, my grades improved and I completed high school with acceptable, though certainly not outstanding, grades.

While in high school, I had my first experience of breaking out from my shyness. It was here I learned that I had the gift of humor; I could tell jokes with a straight face and hold the attention of a crowd. Also, I would impersonate people—Billy Graham, of course, but also Dr. Henry Hildebrand, president of the school. His thick German accent made him an easy target for humor.

One day, dozens of students were congregated in the community washroom area of the boys' dorm, and I was doing a couple of lines I had practiced. What I did not realize was that Dr. Hildebrand had walked into the washroom behind me just as I was impersonating him, carefully delivering my rehearsed speech. The students gasped, but I had no idea why. I wrongly assumed that they were laughing at me. When I turned and saw President Hildebrand, I made up the first alibi that came to mind: I pretended that I was just giving a random speech and now quickly chose to end it by walking over to a window, inviting others to join me in looking outside. He detected my ruse, had a good laugh, and years later we joked about the incident. He also wrote to me when I was in seminary, asking me to return to Briercrest to teach in

51

the Bible department, and I accepted his invitation. And then, about two years before his death, he wrote asking if I'd speak at his funeral service, which I had the honor of doing in February 2006.

I WILL BE A PREACHER

Back in those days, this Christian high school had a policy of having all senior students preach a fifteen-minute message in chapel. This would be my first time to preach, and I had nowhere to turn for sermon material. But the previous summer, while working out on the farm, I came across a book by Billy Graham (who else?) titled *Peace With God.* I was impressed with what he had written about Moses, who turned from the treasures of this world to serve God. I took many of his thoughts, added some of my own, and wrote out my sermon on about a half-dozen pages. I memorized my message word for word and delivered it with ease in about fifteen minutes, ending with the words of the song:

> Must I be carried to the skies on flowery beds of ease,
> While others fought to win the prize and sailed through bloody seas?
> Since I must fight if I would reign, increase my courage, Lord.
> I'll bear the toil, endure the pain, supported by Thy Word.

There was no doubt in my mind that I had found my calling. I preached with a sense of confidence that this was the vocation for which I was born. The desire to preach born within me as a child was confirmed. Thereafter, I knew that somewhere, somehow, I'd end up being a preacher.

WITNESSING TO WHOEVER WOULD LISTEN

During my three years at this Christian high school, I made lifelong friends, among them Bob Parschauer, who later became an evangelist with Word of Life in Germany. While still in high school, we decided to accept an invitation to drive north to his home in Middle Lake, Saskatchewan, and take the service in his home church. Bob led the singing, and I had a new sermon that centered on the two thieves crucified with Jesus; I pointed out that they are symbolic of the whole human race, either believing or disbelieving on Christ.

I've always appreciated Bob's friendship and his passionate desire to see people come to faith in Christ. On the return trip from his home church to our campus, we decided to stop at a Catholic church that was on our route and talk to the priest about salvation. We saw a man working in the churchyard and asked where the priest was. He replied, "I know I don't look like a priest right now, but I am the priest of this parish." We invited him into the car so we could ask him some questions. Bob sat at the wheel, the priest in the front passenger side, and I was in the backseat.

"We'd like to know how we can be sure we will go to heaven," we began. He looked out of the windshield and said, "If you are a friend of God, you will make it, and if you aren't then you won't." Fair enough. Our next question: "How do we become a friend of God?" At this point he launched into a discussion about church attendance, Mass, etc.—but we kept pressing the concept of assurance: How can we know we will go to heaven? Then we quoted verses about assurance such as 1 John 5:12.

"Are you Bible school students?" he asked.

"No, we are just high school students, but we hope to go to Bible school someday."

"Well, if you are just high school students, I'd hate to have to talk with you after you have been to Bible school."

To this day, Bob Parschauer still serves with Word of Life here in the United States, exuding the same tireless enthusiasm for ministry and evangelism he had in high school. In April 2014, I flew down to Florida to speak at the funeral of his dear wife, Betts.

High school also gave me my first opportunity to witness to my faith in Christ on street corners. Several friends and I would hitchhike to the nearby town of Moose Jaw to hand out tracts on the street corners. We argued with Jehovah's Witnesses, warned drunks of hell, and prayed with anyone who would let us. We even had the nerve to enter bars and give out tracts. On one occasion the bartender called the police, insisting that we were "keeping people from entering his bar." That wasn't true, of course; we were just standing at the door handing out literature. When the police came, we innocently told them that the bartender must have been referring to someone else. The cops told us to just be sure that we stayed clear of the door so as not to discourage patrons from entering.

I often spent Sunday afternoons with a friend of mine preparing messages, and then we'd preach them in an empty classroom. Hokey though it seems, we would pretend that we were speaking to thousands of people (the Billy Graham syndrome) and would even go through the motions of giving an invitation. I still have some of the notes from those sermons, written with the scrawl of a high school student, devoid of a serious outline, a mixture of some of my ideas and ideas gleaned from other preachers. I was helped by taking notes whenever a special speaker visited in chapel, or when the school's Bible conference was in progress.

PROVIDENTIAL GUIDANCE

It was toward the end of my senior year of high school that I experienced providential guidance I would come to understand only later. It was quite common for high school graduates to transition from the high school to the Bible school department since they were on the same campus. The principal of the high school encouraged me to fill out an application for a scholarship to enter the Bible school the next fall. So I picked up the application and tucked it in my schoolbag, with the intention of completing the details. But when I sat down to fill it out, I could get no further than writing my name on the top of the page; it was as if there was an invisible hand that kept me from filling it out. I simply sat at my desk unable to write a single word.

I did not know that I was on the verge of making a destiny decision. Some of the decisions we make are not consequential, but as I sat in that classroom, I did not know that I was at a fork in the road that would determine my future. Where I would go to seminary, whom I would marry, and eventually, whether or not I'd end up in Chicago— all of that was at stake and I knew none of it.

I was puzzled. Many of my friends who had graduated with me from high school were applying to attend the Bible department of the school in the fall. Why would God not allow me to attend with them? I was told that if I just filled out this application, I'd be guaranteed a scholarship that would lower the cost. Why this resounding *no* to filling out a simple sheet of questions? God had His reasons, but I did not know or understand them at the time.

A few of my friends, among them a friend named Paul Moninger, had received a catalog from the Winnipeg Bible College, and was encouraging me to attend there with him. I listened to him only half seriously, though his reasons were compelling: we would have more opportunities to preach if we attended a Bible school in the downtown of a big city; and second, Winnipeg Bible College offered a degree, a bachelor of theology, that could be used as a stepping-stone to attend a seminary (at that time Briercrest was resolute in not granting degrees, insisting that an academic emphasis might detract from the more important purpose of developing a heart for God).

Now that I had no freedom in my spirit to return to Briercrest, I began to look at Winnipeg more seriously and filled out an application. My parents were perplexed as to why I would want to go to Bible school so far from home when I was already acquainted with Briercrest, which was much closer. But they were generally supportive. We had an unofficial agreement: if I worked on the farm during the summer, they would pay for my Bible college (and eventually seminary) education.

Since I could not complete the application for Briercrest and was accepted at Winnipeg, the decision was made. That was the easy part. Getting used to the school and life in the big city was challenging, but God was leading in ways I did not expect. In Winnipeg I would meet a man who would be used by God to direct my steps on an unexpected path.

WINNIPEG, HERE WE COME

When Paul and I unpacked our bags at Winnipeg Bible College, we had every reason to believe we had made a huge mistake. This was a small school with a student body of perhaps seventy-five students—very different from the hundreds at Briercrest. The faculty was very small; some were local pastors who taught a course or two in various disciplines. The words of a classmate back at Briercrest haunted me: "If you are going to go to Winnipeg, you will regret it!" She was right, I thought.

Worse, we were lonely—very lonely. At Briercrest, I was well known as the campus comedian and the preacher boy whom some believed

had promise. Here no one had ever heard our names. We were nobod-
ies in a small school in a large city. I shall never forget being awakened
frequently my first night there with the sirens of ambulances haunting
the wide busy streets that were close to the school. Was it even safe to
go outside? Who could drive in such a torrent of traffic? And, were the
school's buildings secure?

On the second or third day, Paul and I were mourning our fate,
when a brilliant idea hit us: Bible school at Briercrest began a week
later than the school in Winnipeg. We could pack our bags, catch a bus
home on the weekend, and still make it to Briercrest for the start of
classes! Surely the school would open its arms to us, even at such a late
date. Just the thought lifted our spirits.

The question was: Did we have the nerve to just up and leave? Once
again, God did not let us cop out of His plan. We simply did not have
peace about returning to Briercrest, though we wanted badly to do so.
Besides, at the end of the first week, we had made some friends, and
we began to think that maybe we would "stick it out for a semester or
a year" and then return to Briercrest the next fall. As it was, we stayed
for all three years, just as God willed.

WHEN TWO SERMONS EQUAL ONE

When I came back to Regina, the city in which my parents now had
a home, the pastor of the Christian and Missionary Alliance Church,
Reverend Orthner—bless him—would occasionally ask me to speak in
an evening service. The first time he asked me, I recall my words exactly: "I don't have a sermon thirty minutes long; I only have two short
sermons, about ten minutes each." He said, "Well then, just tie them
together and preach them!"

That week I did use the material from my messages and prepared a message that hung together on the general theme of revival. Once again I was affirmed by the congregation; several people told me later, "You are called to preach." I had the good fortune of having mentors along the way who believed in me, giving me opportunities to speak, and I had laypeople who encouraged me to exercise my gift.

When counseling young men who are wondering whether they are called to the preaching ministry, I always tell them that it is not enough for them to think they are called to preach; if they are called to preach, then people should also be called to listen.

THE BIBLE, AND MORE BIBLE

For two of those three years at Bible college I was the narrator for the Sacred Music Society of Manitoba, a group of singers that practiced all winter and then held concerts in Winnipeg and a few surrounding towns. I was the one who tied the musical ministry together by the recitation of Scripture. Doing this validated the need to memorize large sections of God's Word. That assignment motivated me to keep memorizing.

Because I wanted to preach, and because I had the undeserved reputation of knowing the Bible well, I began to memorize Scripture on my own. Since I would return home during the summers to work on the farm, I had many leisure hours to memorize chapters and whole books of the Bible. I made an agreement with myself: I would not graduate from Bible college unless I could quote the entire gospel of John by memory.

My method was this: I would read through the gospel of John every three days (seven chapters a day) during the school year. Then when I returned home for the summers, I would memorize large chunks of the text and recite what I had learned while riding on the tractor, plowing the fields, or doing other farmwork. Evenings would be spent memorizing what would be quoted and requoted the next day. Once I

Memorized :-

even brought my Bible onto the tractor, though that really wasn't fea-
sible. When I returned to Bible college, I tried to keep up with what I
learned, though there were many lapses.

The most discouraging part of the process was when I had to re-
learn what I had previously memorized. However, during the Christmas vacation of 1962, I paced the floor in my bedroom at home and
recited all twenty-one chapters of John's gospel in two hours and fifteen
minutes! I continued my memorization during the summers when I
returned home from seminary, and one afternoon I quoted Scripture
for four-and-one-half hours on the tractor without repeating myself. In
addition to John, I could quote Romans, Ephesians, Philippians, and
Hebrews, and ten of the psalms. Although I can't quote these passages
today, the Scriptures I memorized often come back to me and have
been of great help in my ministry throughout the years.

It would be tempting to say that the reason I memorized so many
chapters of the Bible was because I loved it so much. I have to confess
that there were other motivations. Remember, I thought of myself as a
preacher boy, and I was anxious to impress others with my knowledge.
This explains why, in those days, I often preached without notes and
without opening my Bible. I could guide the congregation through the
passage verse by verse, with their Bibles open while mine was closed.

This idea of preaching with a closed Bible came to me when I heard
the Reverend Franklin Logsdon preach at the Christian and Missionary Alliance Church in my hometown of Regina in 1962. He never
looked at a note or his Bible as he guided the congregation through
chapter after chapter of either the Old or New Testament. I thought, if
he could know the Bible that well, then so could I!

And there's more to this story. Dr. Logsdon had been the pastor
of The Moody Church in Chicago for eighteen months after the famous preacher Harry Ironside resigned. Of course, at the time, I didn't

dream that I would follow in his steps and become the pastor of the same church. Years later, I invited Dr. Logsdon to speak at The Moody Church, and I told him about the impact he had had on my life when he had visited my home church years earlier.

THANK YOU, DR. TOWNS

Winnipeg Bible College faced a crisis of leadership during the first two years of my studies there. The president and the board apparently did not "see eye to eye," and even the students felt the tension. When the president resigned, Mr. Affleck, a quiet man with a tender heart, became acting president. He served well, but let it be known that he would only take this responsibility during the interim, and the board was to be looking for a permanent replacement. After several attempts, a new president was found.

Elmer Towns was only twenty-eight years old when he assumed the presidency of the Winnipeg Bible College in the fall of my senior year. He was energetic, knowledgeable, and simply did not understand the meaning of the words, "It can't be done." Within weeks, he outlined a plan for the school's future, engaged the board about the direction of the school, and clearly communicated that the school needed to be more attuned to the times. I'm not sure what the response of the board was, but I do know that Elmer remained president for only four years. Personally, I believe his leadership paved the way for the future expansion of the school.

Shortly after he arrived, I impersonated him in a faculty/student skit. That I had hit the mark was confirmed by his wife who leaned over and whispered to Elmer, "That is exactly how you talk and act." Elmer told me later that the skit broke the ice; he now knew he had been accepted by the students. He reasoned, quite correctly, that I would not have mimicked him if he wasn't liked by us.

Elmer had a direct impact on my life in two ways. First, he modeled how to teach with enthusiasm and confidence. For him the classroom was not just a place of learning, but of transformation—a place where students were challenged to be all that they could be. He helped light a fuse within me, a desire to think big thoughts about how God might use me.

Elmer influenced my life in another way: he encouraged me to attend Dallas Theological Seminary, the school from which he had recently graduated. He told me, "You will never reach your potential unless you get better training." I think I'd heard of Dallas Theological Seminary, but knew little about the school.

After graduation from Bible college in the spring of 1962, I returned to Regina and attended the University of Saskatchewan to study humanities. This year of study was a requirement in order for me to receive an undergraduate degree from the Winnipeg Bible College that would qualify me for entering Dallas Seminary. With that behind me, Dallas was now in my sights.

Perhaps it was because a degree from a Bible college was suspect, or perhaps it was because my grades at the university were not spectacular, that Dallas Seminary would only accept me on probation. And, most important, Elmer Towns wrote a letter of recommendation to the seminary on my behalf.

Years later, our paths crossed briefly on several occasions, and Elmer would have an impact in my life once more. But that story must wait.

GOD'S LEADING MADE CLEAR

Only now did I begin to understand why God did not let me complete that application for Briercrest! If I had attended there, I would not have met Elmer Towns, nor would I have had a degree to enter Dallas Seminary. If I'd gone to Briercrest, I probably would have gone into a pastorate somewhere on the Canadian prairies, and my life would have taken a different route. But it was to be at Dallas where decisions would be made that would direct the trajectory of my life.

Winnipeg Bible College and Elmer Towns were my link to a seminary where I would continue to overcome my shyness and deepen my knowledge of the Bible through courses in Greek, Hebrew, apologetics, and theology. More important, there in the Southern "Bible Belt" I would meet the woman I would eventually marry.

God was beginning to paint a picture but I could see only the first strokes of His brush. I had no idea what the final portrait would be.

CHAPTER 4

Dallas, Racism, and the Death of a President

❧

D allas is hot even in September.

I arrived at the seminary a few days early because I took the opportunity to hitch a ride with a friend who was en route to John Brown University in Arkansas. From there I took a bus to Dallas, and a cab to the seminary.

For the most part, the campus was deserted, meals were not yet being served, and I was assigned to live in a small house just off the premises. I used the few dollars I had for food and waited anxiously for the students to arrive. I resented my assigned quarters in a house off campus. Within a few days I had a roommate named Allen, a fine chap, but for some reason we never formed a close friendship. He was a football fan, knew all the scores of the college football teams, and followed the teams in the growing NFL. I was surprised at how much attention football received in the South.

But during those first weeks, I felt very lonely. I was, after all, still a farmboy at heart, from the prairies of Canada, living in a strange land,

and so far from home. Thankfully, I met a few other students who be-friended me and assured me that I would soon adjust to seminary life once classes began and everything was in high gear. On at least two or three evenings I walked down Swiss Avenue, next to the seminary, cry-ing to myself. Yes, I was lonely, but I was also afraid of failing the course work. I had heard rumors of how difficult it was to study Hebrew, and I had long since forgotten the bit of Greek I had learned in Bible school. I called out to God to help me and to not bring me to disgrace.

Several times in the last few years, I've been asked to speak at the seminary, and each time I deliberately walk down Swiss Avenue giving praise to God for all He has done in my life since those fearful, lonely days in September 1963.

Along with the challenge of my new surroundings, I experienced an extraordinary sense of the presence of God. In those early days, week-ends were particularly difficult, but I would return to my room to pray, and there I would so sense that God was with me that I could scarcely contain the sheer joy. In fact, I thanked God for setting me apart, just so that I could learn that He could make up for my loneliness.

My sister Esther, bless her, was the first to send me a letter. She knew I would probably be lonely and mailed the letter almost as soon as I left for Dallas. I not only read it a couple of times, but carried it in my back pocket for several days. Soon after, she would become a missionary in Africa and told me that she liked to receive mail from home. I wish I had been as faithful in writing to her as she was in writing to me!

I adjusted well to the seminary classes. However, I felt intimidated by the "famous" professors I now saw almost every day. Men like Drs. Ryrie, Unger, Walvoord, and Hendricks were known to me through their books, and now I had the opportunity to talk with them. Again, thanks to my shy disposition, I seldom asked questions in class, and for the most part, I just minded my business, studying as hard as I could.

Soon I discovered that seminary was not beyond my capability. In fact, with some exceptions, I was surprised at how manageable it was. My fear of failure was unfounded. In the end I graduated with honors.

WHITES ONLY

It was during those early days that I was introduced to the racism that still permeated the South in the early sixties. As we walked down the streets of Dallas, we would see "Whites Only" signs in restaurants, clothing stores, and laundromats. The nearby cleaners where we seminarians would take our shirts had a "Whites Only" sign, and nary was a word said about it even in the seminary. The civil rights battles were raging throughout the South; George Wallace was standing in a doorway at the University of Alabama to make sure that no black student would enter.

Sadly, racism existed even in the churches; there were Sunday school meetings for African Americans, but the worship services were all too often filled with only white worshipers. Although Dallas Seminary's policy was to accept all qualified students, I don't recall an African American student on campus when I was there.

Today the seminary is intentionally racially diverse. Every year the present president, Dr. Mark Bailey, publically reaffirms an institutional apology for all real and any perceived prejudice that students past or present have experienced, which "may have discouraged others from applying and thereby kept full reconciliation and mutual respect from being what it always should be—the biblical order of the day. May we who study and serve at DTS always celebrate our family identity and unity in Christ as the truest definition of our community."

Dallas Seminary is fully integrated. It's wonderful to see students from all parts of the world welcomed and encouraged to attend DTS.

THE PRESIDENT'S BEEN SHOT!

Kennedy

The fall of my freshman year, 1963, my sister Ruth, her husband, Richard, and their children stopped in Dallas to visit me on their way to Mexico. They were missionaries with Wycliffe Bible Translators in the Cuicateco Indian tribe 250 miles south of Mexico City. My sister Esther was also with them, wanting to see their work firsthand.

I visited with them in a motel near the seminary the evening before President and Mrs. Kennedy were scheduled to visit the city, and we agreed to have lunch together the next day. We talked about the impending visit of the president and the various attitudes toward him in the city of Dallas.

The next day began like any ordinary morning of classes. But at about 11:30, word was spreading that the president had been shot while riding in his motorcade. Afternoon classes were canceled and students and faculty huddled beside their radios waiting for the latest news. The initial news was that he had been wounded, but there were conflicting reports about the extent of the injuries.

When Richard and Ruth came to pick me up, we stopped at a cafeteria for lunch and asked the cashier if she had heard the latest news. "He's gone," she said, looking away to hold back the tears. When we left the restaurant, we saw people weeping openly in the streets. Hours later we were relieved to learn that the Dallas police had apprehended one Lee Harvey Oswald who apparently was the perpetrator of this ghastly deed.

Only those who were in Dallas at the time can appreciate the shock that Kennedy's assassination was to the city. The mood was surreal, eerie, and somber. On Sunday, many of us students went to hear Dr. Criswell preach at the First Baptist Church. He spoke about the tragedy, emphasizing the brevity of life, the need for us to realize that our world is filled with evil, and that all men would have to someday give an account to God.

When we came out of church, more unbelievable news awaited us. The radio blared the news that Jack Ruby had just shot Lee Harvey Oswald, supposedly to spare Jackie Kennedy the agony of a trial. Surely this was stranger than fiction.

The Dallas police were severely criticized for transporting a handcuffed Oswald to his permanent jail cell in the presence of the media and, apparently, with lax security. This strange sequence of events would mean that Oswald's guilt would never be proven in court and that conspiracy theories about Kennedy's death would abound. A recent Secret Service recruit told me that while in training, they had to take an entire course on the Kennedy assassination. In the end, no one theory of how it happened has answered all the questions. Thus, fifty years after the event, conspiracy theories of various kinds still flourish. This is truly "the story that won't go away."

As for Oswald, not even the minister showed up for his burial, and members of the press acted as pallbearers. Many years later, Rebecca and I saw Oswald's grave when we were visiting a relative who lived near the cemetery where he was buried. We were surprised at the well-traveled path that led to his grave, probably because others like us wanted to be able to say that "we were there." On his tombstone is but one word: Oswald.

You might expect me to say that everyone mourned the death of the president, but that wouldn't be true. It's one thing for us to look back at Kennedy's life and see the charm, the elegance, and the memorable speeches given by him throughout his brief tenure in office. But remember, many people thought that he had stolen the presidency from Nixon (with the help of Mayor Daley in Chicago), creating plenty of political enemies for Kennedy.

Add to this the fact that he was promoting a civil rights agenda (meaning, among other things, that the "Whites Only" signs would have to disappear), and given the Kennedy wealth and rumors of sexual trysts, you can understand that many people disliked (shall we say *hated*) the Kennedys and all they stood for. In Dallas there was consternation that a president could be assassinated, but for many, instead of grief, there was relief. To my dismay, even in the late seventies, the pastor of a well-known church told me over breakfast, "Oswald did this country some good."

Classes resumed at the seminary after Kennedy's funeral, but the city of Dallas, wondering how an assassination could happen here, was overtaken by what I would call a sense of collective introspection and embarrassment. Now outsiders spoke of the city (unfairly in my opinion) as "the murder capital of the world." Even those who disliked the president agreed that his murder was a tragic example of a world run amuck.

Piles of flowers littered the grassy knoll where the motorcade had traveled. Some of us drove past the place of this tragedy every Sunday on the way to church. And in recent years I've visited the museum at the Dallas Bookroom Depository that is dedicated to the events of that fateful day.

I still recall the lead article in the *Dallas Morning News* the day before the president and his wife arrived. The writer detailed the measures that had been taken to protect the president and added, "If possible the Secret Service would have checked the very air the president and his wife would breathe." The Secret Service had made all the preparations humanly possible, but when the clouds parted and the sun began to shine, it was the president's idea to ride in an open motorcade—and the rest is history. If it had been raining in Dallas that morning, the entire course of American history might have been different.

MINISTRY AND BLESSINGS

In my senior year, a well-known preacher and professor, Dr. Haddon Robinson, asked me to be one of several assistants who would help him teach homiletics to underclassmen. Our responsibility was to critique the preaching of fellow students in a small group setting. One of those in my group was Duane Litfin, who would finish seminary, graduate from Oxford, return to the seminary to teach, and finally, in 1993, become the president of Wheaton College. (When he was in Dallas, he and his wife also invited me to their home on Thanksgiving Day, a gracious gesture greatly appreciated by single seminary students.) Under his leadership, Wheaton prospered with a renewed commitment to the Scriptures and evangelism. Now I can say, "I knew him when . . ."

Dr. Joseph Stowell, president of Moody Bible Institute for seventeen years, was also an underclassman. And although I did not know him well at the time, he clearly demonstrated the gift of leadership. He became the pastor of Highland Park Baptist Church in Michigan, and when he became the president of Moody Bible Institute in 1987, I was on hand to wish him God's blessing. His natural gifts, combined with a fervent desire to serve the Lord, furthered the strong legacy of spiritual leadership at the Institute.

Dr. Stowell sometimes joked that in seminary, the three of us got together and we agreed, "Duane, you take Wheaton; Erwin, you take The Moody Church; and Joe, you take Moody Bible Institute!" Certainly no one of sound mind would have predicted that someday God would give the three of us such positions of responsibility. In 2005, Dr. Stowell resigned to take a position at the Harvest Bible Chapel in the Chicago area. Currently he serves as president of Cornerstone University in Grand Rapids. We continue to be close friends.

I was also a classmate with Dr. David Jeremiah, whose radio and television ministry, *Turning Point,* has made him known throughout the country. Don Wyrtzen of music fame was an underclassman who played the piano for chapel as well as for skits and parties.

ENCOURAGEMENT ALONG THE WAY

I usually sat in the front row during the classes at seminary, saying very little, yet attracting attention outside of the classroom through my preaching and impersonations. One day Dr. Hendricks asked if he could see me after class. I felt intimidated in his presence because of his expertise and perceptive comments. I breathed more easily when he said he simply wanted to encourage me. He said he appreciated my "teachable spirit" and that he noticed that I had some abilities that would be used of the Lord. I walked away pleasantly surprised that he saw such potential in me.

Throughout the years, we have had many times of warm fellowship. Sometimes we have spoken together at the same conference, or we would meet at Moody Bible Institute's Founder's Week. "Prof," as he was affectionately called, always reached out, encouraging me in the ministry. Indeed, he wrote the foreword to one of my first books, *Failure: The Backdoor to Success.* When he died early in 2013, I could truly say that his impact on my life was immeasurable. Not merely his teaching, wonderful as it was, but his personal encouragement.

As in Bible school, I now was known for my impersonation of Billy Graham, but I also added Dr. Hendricks and the well-known scholar, Merrill F. Unger, to my repertoire. In fact, sometimes I would do a one-man skit, working in all three. Dr. Unger was at first apprehensive when he heard that he'd been impersonated, but after we met, he accepted it all in good humor. In fact, he autographed a copy of his *Unger's Bible Handbook* to me, in honor of "Erwin Unger Lutzer."

For reasons that are unclear to me, I was elected president of the student body in my senior year. Dr. Hendricks was the student advisor who sat in on our meetings, trying to help us keep on track and improve student-faculty relations. Whatever accomplishments we made (if there were any) have long faded from my memory. But one thing does stand out in my mind: we students made arrangements to purchase the first photocopy machine for the seminary. We called it by its trade name—a Xerox. What a blessing to have it in time for us seniors to duplicate our dissertations!

THE CONFUSING WILL OF GOD

After seminary, what? That is a question every senior has in the back of his mind as graduation draws near. A year before graduation, I had received a letter from Dr. Henry Hildebrand asking me to return to Briercrest to teach in the Bible department in the fall after graduation. I felt honored to receive the invitation. After all, this was the same campus where I had attended high school; my brothers and sisters had graduated from the Bible school, and now I, the youngest in the Lutzer family, would come back to teach. It sounded like "homeboy makes good." So I said *yes*.

But as graduation approached, I regretted my decision. I had become accustomed to life in a big city; in the South, none of my friends had ever heard of Saskatchewan, much less a school called Briercrest. When I told my friends where I would be going to teach, many of them wondered if the place was actually on a map. What's more, Dr. Ryrie had encouraged me to stay at Dallas and work toward a ThD; it was generally agreed that a doctorate is needed if one is going to become a respected professor.

But a promise is a promise. A year earlier I had accepted Dr.

Hildebrand's invitation, and I determined I would make the best of the experience. So I was headed back to Saskatchewan, but not before I would experience the most difficult emotional convulsion of my life.

In my final semester of seminary, I went through the anguish that love can bring. God was still caring for me, but I couldn't see His hand until months later.

Before leaving Dallas, I would undergo a journey into emotional confusion and darkness.

CHAPTER 5

If This Be Love

M̲y first serious romance took place in my last semester in seminary. Back in high school I experienced the normal attachments;
I liked one girl or another, but it never progressed to becoming a serious
relationship. In Bible school, there was a secretary I found attractive, so
one day I got on my knees and asked God a simple question: Is this the
woman for me? As clear as if I heard a voice from heaven, the answer
was *no*. How I wish God always led me with such certainty!

Little did I realize the indescribable agony a relationship with a
young woman in Dallas would bring. Even now, nearly fifty years later,
I still remember the confusion and pain of those few months. Here is
the story as best I remember it.

I met a young woman, whom I shall call Carol, at a singles party
sponsored by Scofield Church, where I attended in my senior year.
She was sitting on the floor, listening to a devotional given by one of
the students. I was nearby, so we struck up a conversation. She told
me about the trials she was going through: a dysfunctional family (no,
she didn't use the word), a fruitless job search, and the heartbreak of a
past relationship. She was the only Christian in her family and did not

know what the future held. The only thing that mattered, she said, is that the Lord would take care of her. The God who saved her was the God who would lead her.

If there is such a thing as love at first sight, this was it. I was deeply impressed by this young woman who seemed so sincere, and to whom I felt such a connection. I had always had a sense that the woman I would marry would come from the United States, and this was my last year of seminary! During Christmas break, I went to visit my sister Ruth and her husband, Richard, in Mexico. I recall saying to my sister, "I have met a young woman for whom I would be willing to die . . ."

The problem, however, is that a good friend of mine living on the same floor in the dormitory, whom I shall call Brian, was dating Carol. In fact, there were times I saw them together at Scofield Church, leaving my heart torn within me. Brian knew of my love for Carol, but he had no idea the extent to which I felt committed to her. Their relationship seemed casual, but they were together all too often for me.

There was only one thing for me to do: give the matter to God and trust His will to be done. After all, He knew my pain, He had a plan, and He could easily cause one relationship to end and another to begin. Either God is God or He is not. If He is not, then He is unworthy of my allegiance; if He is God, then nothing is too hard for Him. *Nothing.*

GOD'S WILL APPARENTLY MADE CLEAR

Weeks went by, then one evening Brian came into my room and said, "Erwin, I know you like Carol and I'm here to tell you that you can date her because we broke up tonight." Finally, the will of God was being done on earth even as it is in heaven!

Within a day or two, I called Carol and we began our dating relationship. I discovered that she too felt strongly about me from the first time we met at the Scofield party. But she had assumed that I, student body president et al., would never be interested in her. Now that she discovered differently, she confirmed my fervent belief that this was a relationship "made in heaven." I would tell my friends, "Our love story is like a page from the Bible—nothing less than God making His will as clear as day."

We spent as much time together as we could. I borrowed a car from a freshman, a seminary student whom I knew during my days at Winnipeg Bible College, so that we could go out at least once or twice a week. Here was a love that would last, a relationship I thought was confirmed by God Himself.

And then all hell broke loose.

THE DARK TUNNEL

I found myself waking up in the morning, almost unable to get out of bed, burdened by a heavy weight of depression that simply would not go away. Sometimes my world was so dark, so emotionally draining, that I wondered how I'd make it through the day. One Sunday I told a friend, "It is as if I have two rivers within me, going opposite directions, and there is no relief." I clearly remember thinking that if I had to live the rest of my life this way, ending my life would have to be an option.

When I told Carol about my struggles, she was unmoved. "Take as long as you need . . . God has shown me that we are meant for each other." She told me that she had read Genesis 12 in her devotions, and God showed her that just like Abraham, she too would have to leave her home country (the USA) for another country (Canada), and that we should not lose sight of the way we met. God was in our relationship, come what may. Meanwhile, I was forced to entertain the unwelcome thought that maybe we would have to end our relationship just so that I would have a few hours of peace.

What confused me was that there were days when the depression would be gone and the "sun would shine." I spoke to a counselor who said, "Erwin, you were brought up in a sheltered environment. You have not had a serious relationship before; the thought of marriage is scary for anyone, but especially for you. This is just the normal response to someone who is coming down to a decision about marriage."

He was wrong, but at the time that made sense to me.

I was convinced that the relationship was obviously from God, so it had to stay on track—come what may. But the emotional turmoil would not subside. This, I thought, must have been what Gethsemane was like: nothing but unrelenting depression, hopeless distress, and emotional turbulence of the worst sort. If hell was half this bad, I feared for people who were headed in that direction.

Mustering all the willpower within me, I met with Carol and told her that I had no option: if I wanted to retain my sanity, we would have to end our relationship. She accepted it courageously, and said wistfully, "If I don't see you again, maybe we will say 'hi' to each other in the choir in heaven." I wept with all my soul as I said goodbye. Not so much for myself, but for a young woman whose heart I'd just broken.

If only that were the end of this story!

MAKING A BAD SITUATION WORSE

Weeks later, I made a foolish decision that would only prolong my own agony and increase Carol's. Within a day or two after the breakup, the depression was gone. I was able to function normally, attend classes, do assignments. I had time to reflect on what happened and thought that surely God would not have led me to this woman just to mock me.

Had I not sought His will? Did she not seek His will? Why would Brian have walked into my room that evening and said, "Erwin, you can date Carol"? Perhaps my depression was from the Devil and not from God.

A week or so later, I called her to say that, as far as I was concerned, the relationship was back on track. She was not surprised because, after all, God had shown her it would all work out in the end. Needless to say, the depression returned, and it appeared more manageable. She attended my graduation ceremonies at the seminary on the evening of May 17, 1967, and I left with some friends for Canada the next day. We parted on uncertain terms, but we believed that God would show us the way.

This would be my last summer helping my father on the farm in Canada, and I'd be teaching nearby at Briercrest in the fall. Carol and I exchanged letters and occasionally talked on the telephone. Obviously it was difficult for our relationship to progress at a distance of 1,500 miles. Either we had to marry or break up once again. Despite the difficulties of the past, I couldn't escape the conclusion that God had led us together.

THE FATEFUL VISIT

I invited Carol to visit me in Canada to meet my family near the end of June. My parents were excited about meeting the woman who just might become their daughter-in-law. But the days she spent with us were awkward with no rapport on either side. My parents urged me to not marry her, believing that she did not have the qualities needed for the wife of a pastor or teacher. My father put it even more strongly, saying that if we were married, his affection for me would be removed.

The evening before Carol was scheduled to fly back to Dallas, I prayed one last time, "God, if this woman is not for me, throw a brick at me to get my attention!" When I was scarcely able to get up out of bed the next morning because of the depression that raged in my soul, I knew that "the brick" had arrived. In retrospect, I felt as though I was digging out from a whole pile of bricks. God had been throwing them in my direction since the first week I began our relationship way back in Dallas.

Carol and I visited the Parliament Buildings in Regina en route to the airport. When we parted, I knew that this would be the last time we would see each other. She acknowledged that our relationship had been too difficult and that God had thrown me "one brick too many." In the days that followed, we exchanged a few letters, then in a final phone call we wished one another well as we went our separate ways.

Months later, a mutual friend brought me up-to-date on Carol's subsequent decisions. Without going into detail, let me simply say that she apparently struggled with various emotional challenges and entered a questionable marriage relationship. Of course, there is no way for me to know whether the ordeal of our breakup played a part in her troubled future.

Quite possibly, if we had married, I wouldn't be in the ministry today. My parents were right: Carol did not have the abilities and stability needed for the special responsibilities of a pastor's wife. Even more serious, however, she suffered from her own emotional distresses that were probably rooted in her dysfunctional family. She had been on medication for depression, but I missed the warning signs.

I have often prayed for her and truly hope that she has had a productive and fulfilled life. I know she loved God and desired His will; she was a woman who wanted to bless others and to invest her life for Christ.

UNANSWERED QUESTIONS

I've often pondered several questions that grow out of my story. First, does God lead people together, although it is not His will for them to marry? The answer, I believe, is *yes*. I was helped by the story of how God gave Abraham a son Isaac and then asked him to kill him on Mount Moriah. Although Isaac's life was spared by God's direct intervention, the principle applies: God brings people into our lives and then takes them from us to test our faith. Does this person mean more to us than God? Only a separation will reveal the truth.

Second, I am grateful that God stayed with me through my ordeal, and would not let me marry Carol. But I have often puzzled why He did not prevent other people from mismatched marriages even as He had done for me. I know couples who live with deep regret and "buyer's remorse" because they married a person with whom they must now live in conflict and unhappiness. Some have been divorced; others live lives of quiet desperation wishing they could find an honorable exit out of the marriage.

I've known men who had the same calling to preach as I, but have not been able to fulfill their vision because of an unhappy or emotionally crippled wife. Of course, there are many Christian women whose lives have been ruined by marrying an insensitive or even immoral man. My point is simple: Why does God not keep all of His children from foolish decisions, just as He did for me?

If you ask me why God has so graciously intervened in my life, I cannot answer. All that I know is that I have lived with His undeserved favor; I have felt that God's hand was on my life, perhaps because of the prayers of my parents. This is not the only time He has put a roadblock in my path to keep me on course.

Finally, I've questioned, "How we can determine the will of God in the decisions we make?" From my own personal experience, I've learned that the will of God often can't be determined by circumstances, by hunches, by feelings, or by Scripture quoted out of context. I've also learned that we can be easily led astray by some people, but that God can lead us through the wise counsel of others.

If I could shout this advice from the housetops I would do so. I would repeat for all to hear: IT IS POSSIBLE TO BE IN LOVE WITH SOMEONE YOU SHOULD NOT MARRY! This applies to both the unmarried and the married. Yes, a married man or woman can "fall in love" with someone other than their spouse, resulting in adultery and often divorce. Or they can have an "emotional affair" with someone other than their spouse. The consequences are heartbreaking. We must remember that the moment we say "I do," the person we have married is now God's exclusive will for us.

As for singles, I tell them, "Please give God a good chance to break up your relationship; please don't plunge ahead disregarding all of the warning signs. And if your soul is distressed over your impending marriage, end the relationship. Better the pain of a breakup than the pain of a miserable marriage." Like the old adage says, "It is better to want what you don't have than to have what you don't want!"

As pastors at The Moody Church, we are protective of singles in our congregation. We strongly discourage marriage if we see red flags in the relationship; we won't perform a wedding if we believe the marriage, for one reason or another, is either unwise or unbiblical.

Meanwhile, God was preparing someone else for me to marry. She'd be a woman of strength who would compensate for my weaknesses. She endured a difficult childhood in a dysfunctional family but has proven that God's grace and mercy can heal and restore. Through a variety of circumstances God led us together, and we've had a rewarding journey.

GOD SMILES

During my final semester at DTS, every seminary student was expected to bring a date to the senior banquet held every February. Carol had a conflict in her schedule, so with her approval, I asked a young woman named Rebecca, whom I had met in a church several months earlier, to attend the dinner with me. She was a student at Dallas Bible College, and since she was also dating someone, she got permission from her boyfriend to go to this special event. So, obviously, it was clear to all that this was a onetime date.

That night at the banquet we sat at the head table with the president of the seminary, Dr. and Mrs. John Walvoord, and other dignitaries. As the student body president, I had a part in the program. Perhaps by now you have guessed it; I was to supply the humor with my imper-sonation of Billy Graham.

That evening on the drive back to our dormitories, Rebecca told me of her love for the mountains and jokingly suggested that if someday we were to get married we should spend our honeymoon in Colorado. To be sure, it was a lighthearted and whimsical idea. Both of us were involved in our own serious relationships, and we understood that this occasion was only for the benefit of my need to take a date to this high-light of my graduation year.

After that evening, our lives went their separate ways. It would be two years before we'd connect and see each other again. Yet incredibly, this young woman and I would eventually marry and have our honey-moon in Colorado! That night at the banquet, God must have looked down from heaven and smiled.

A new chapter of my life was about to begin.

CHAPTER 6

Marriage, Chicago, and Ministry

❧

My decision to teach at Briercrest Bible College would bring me back to my roots. The school was just a two-hour drive from the farm where I grew up, and less than an hour from Regina, where my parents were now living. It was an honor to be on a par with faculty members I had come to know eight years earlier when I was a high school student on the same campus. Now, with a Master's of Theology on my résumé, I was ready to make my contribution to the educational challenges of this well-known Canadian school.

And yet, I was unsettled in my spirit.

Briercrest is situated in the middle of the southern Saskatchewan prairie, quite literally miles from nowhere. Those who visit the school for the first time are surprised that a school was built at that juncture along the No. 1 highway. After endless miles of flat prairie, suddenly in the distance a tall building appears and then another. Only when you arrive on campus do you realize that a town had grown up around what was, during World War II, an air force base. Now it was totally rebuilt with dormitories and educational buildings.

For someone who had become accustomed to living in Winnipeg and Dallas, it seemed as if I was in a time warp, going back to my early days and regressing to the windswept farmlands where there was no protection from the bitter cold of winter or shelter from the frequent winds during the summer. Be that as it may, I was here, and the challenge of teaching in a Bible college was before me.

Since I was still single, my roommate was another young faculty member, Walter Weiser, who was scheduled to teach pastoral ministry. We lived in one of the suites on campus, took our meals in the dining hall, and spent much of our time discussing what we thought were the big ideas of theology and culture.

STUDYING IN ISRAEL

In 1968, the summer after my first year of teaching, I had the privilege of studying in Israel with Wheaton College. My friend Ray Matheson was attending Wheaton at the time, and we agreed to take advantage of this on-site study program. The previous year (1967), Israel had captured the Old City of Jerusalem in the famous and near-miraculous Six-Day War. After we visited Egypt and Cyprus, Jerusalem became our home base, and we traversed the land without restrictions, even taking a four-day trip to Mt. Sinai, spending the night in St. Catherine's monastery, and climbing to the top of the mountain early the next morning.

We also climbed to the top of Masada along what the ancient historian Josephus referred to as "the snake trail." My body was so dehydrated walking up the steep mountain in 100-plus-degree temperatures that it took about three days for it to rehydrate. In retrospect, it's a wonder that we lived to tell about our experience. Today tourists whiz to the top by cable car, a luxury we never dreamed of way back in 1968.

Dr. Barton Payne, an enthusiastic and humble scholar, was our primary leader and lecturer, crawling into caves, climbing hills, and giving us assignments in archaeology and Old Testament history. I've returned to Israel six times since that memorable summer, but whenever I think of the Holy Land, my mind always goes back to what I learned and saw during those twelve weeks of intensive study and touring.

That fall, after returning from Israel, I taught a second year at Briercrest, wondering what I'd be doing in the years to come. My calling to preach and teach hadn't diminished, but I longed for a greater challenge. I found myself being somewhat bored teaching the same courses and walking in predictable paths. There was something more out there that God wanted me to do, but I didn't know what it was.

A LETTER TO REBECCA

From time to time my mind wandered back to a young woman named Rebecca Hickman, whom I had met while attending church at Polk Street Bible Chapel in Dallas. She was the young woman I took to the Dallas Seminary senior banquet. Now, two years later, I was wondering whatever happened to her—did she marry the young man she'd been dating? Did they become missionaries as they had hoped? I thought back to the fun we had the night she accompanied me to the banquet. We seemed to connect, and I sensed that we were like-minded in our desire to follow and serve God wherever He led us. So I wrote her a note on an airmail form, which basically said that I wondered what she'd been doing since we'd last seen each other. I acknowledged that she might be engaged, married, or otherwise serving the Lord as a single missionary, but if not, would she care to correspond?

A few days later, I was standing in the school post office when a letter from her arrived. Before I read it, I counted the pages. I said to my room-mate Walley, who was standing next to me, "It would not have taken her four pages to say no!" and, as you might guess, the letter was a "*Yes, I'd like to correspond with you!*"

Much to my surprise and delight, she was neither married nor en-gaged, having recently ended the relationship with her longtime boy-friend. After that, we began to write regularly, getting caught up on the past and thinking about the future. So, it was almost two years after my graduation that I'd write a letter and jump-start a relationship.

Only when we reconnected did I learn that Rebecca had attended my seminary graduation ceremony the evening of May 17, 1967. As she and one of her girlfriends drove on a Dallas expressway back to the Dallas Bible College dorm, Rebecca was driving over a rise in the high-way, when she saw a vehicle nearly stopped in the lane ahead of her. When she turned the steering wheel sharply to avoid a collision, the car flipped on its side and skidded down the pavement for a long distance. Incredibly, no car hit hers as the smoking Volkswagen came to a halt in the middle of the expressway. Thankfully, she and her friend escaped serious injury with only bumps and bruises, even though Rebecca had been temporarily knocked out and discovered the next day she had a concussion and a back injury.

Now here we were getting to know each other, and our relationship began to get serious. Both of us only wanted what God had planned for us, and so it was that two very different and unlikely individuals were about to embark on a whirlwind romance and be married. And the rest, as they say, is history.

REBECCA'S STORY

Rebecca was born in Dallas on July 25, 1947, during the time her parents lived in a trailer on the campus of Dallas Theological Seminary. Her father had served in the US Navy for eight years, and her mother had served two years in the air force during World War II. They married in July 1945 and were anxious to settle down, begin a new life, and start a family. But from the beginning, their marriage was filled with much conflict. Anger and regret fueled heated arguments. Vastly different backgrounds, painful events in their lives, and memories of the Depression left them ill-prepared for the challenges of marriage and parenting. They both had unrealistic and unusual expectations, and together came up with unconventional methods of punishment that left emotional and spiritual wounds upon their children . . .

When she was ten, her family of eight moved into a partially finished structure one-half mile off the highway on a dirt road. Though it was 1956, this "house" did not have a flushing toilet or telephone. The only furniture was a kitchen table and chairs and beds—mostly old metal army cots. The only appliances were a refrigerator, a cooking stove, one small heating stove, and a washing machine that drained into one side of a divided utility tub.

The roof leaked in several places, so twenty-gallon metal cans were scattered around the house to catch the dripping water when it rained. This forty-by-forty-foot shack had just one dividing wall. Boxes of clothes, books, and junk created small spaces that became "rooms." Prior to this move, she and her family had lived in a variety of locations, enduring hardship and poverty.

Though her father had attended a seminary program, hoping to go into full-time ministry, her mother's multiple health problems prevented this. She was emotionally and physically unable to take care of six children and the household.

Trying to cope with these difficult circumstances, Rebecca's parents inflicted severe emotional and physical discipline and punishment on their six children for both real and imagined disobedience. Cruel words and actions wounded their spirits and bodies. Poverty, neglect, and abuse produced shame and humiliation in six children. At times Rebecca wore a long-sleeved shirt to hide strap marks on her arms.

At school, she felt out of place without pretty clothes or nice shoes to wear, just hand-me-downs from her older brother or secondhand clothes from Goodwill. One bright spot during those difficult times was that she was smart and could help others with their homework and study questions.

As the oldest daughter, it was her responsibility to cook and wash dishes. She did the laundry and even occasionally cared for the livestock. On top of that, she was expected to take care of her sick mother. Schoolwork had to wait until the early morning hours, when her father woke her to iron his shirt before he left for work. Sometimes she was fortunate enough to get an uninterrupted hour in which she could study and do homework before walking a mile and a half to school (once in a while making it to the highway to ride the school bus). Occasionally, she'd slip from her cot at night to read her Bible by the pilot light of the water heater. She was sustained by the belief that God really did love her and that He had a plan for her life. She believed that He was leading her to become a missionary nurse.

Strangely, in this harsh atmosphere, her parents loved God and taught the children to revere and love the Bible. At times, the children were required to sit quietly and listen to various radio Bible teachers. They attended a small Bible church, and in the summer, the kids loved going to a Christian camp in another state. But no one could have imagined what was going on inside their home. It was a sad and dark secret.

In the fall of 1965, Rebecca began her studies at Dallas Bible College in their missions program and also belonged to one of the singing groups. Coming from a dysfunctional, abusive, and poverty-stricken home, it now seemed that a wonderful world of people and opportunities had opened up to her. A few weeks into the semester she reconnected with a young man named Charles she had known in her early teen years at Bible camp. He was anxious to begin dating, and they enjoyed a developing friendship for the next three months.

But tragedy struck. In late December, Charles invited her to join him, along with her older brother Lewis who was on leave from navy duty, and another good friend for a double date. However, Rebecca was in Dallas and they were in Fort Worth, so she declined since it would be a late evening and she had to work the next day. Later that night, Charles dropped Lewis off at the family home, and as he continued the drive back to Fort Worth, he was killed in a car accident. This sad and shocking loss had a profound effect on Rebecca, and from that moment on she became a very serious Bible student, rededicating her life to God's calling. Months later she began dating a young man committed to becoming a missionary pilot, believing that God's call to the mission field had been reaffirmed. This was the man she had been dating when I took her to the seminary banquet.

During the summer of 1968, Rebecca traveled with a group of young people to Mexico and Central America as part of a missions training program. While in the jungles of Mexico at the Wycliffe Center, she became ill and had several days to think and pray as she sat in a small hut under mosquito netting. God seemed to be asking her to end the relationship with her longtime boyfriend whom she loved. After much prayer and inner struggle, she submitted to what she believed was God's will, and returned to Dallas Bible College to begin her senior year. She wrote her friend a letter explaining how God had led her to make this difficult decision, and mailed it to him near the end of November. Just one week later she received the letter I had written to her on the airmail form; it arrived on December 4, 1968!

The next year in April 1969, I invited Rebecca to fly to Regina to visit me and meet my family. It had been two years since we had seen each other at the seminary banquet, and now after four months of writing to each other, it was time that we met and talked face-to-face. Her visit was very different from the one that Carol had made in 1967. Rebecca was enthusiastic, friendly, and helpful, always alert to the needs of others. Unlike the previous experience, my parents were favorably impressed, and my other family members were drawn to her. I had a growing realization that this indeed might be the woman God had chosen for me. Time would tell.

That summer I had planned to drive to Chicago to take summer school classes in what had been known as "The Winona Lake School of Theology." This summer school had moved from Indiana to Chicago in a vain hope to attract more students and make it more attractive for various well-known professors to come to lecture for a few weeks. There I met Gordon Clark, Clark Pinnock, Carl Henry, and other philosophers who would have a lasting effect on my life.

However, I now had a reason to make a detour. My heart was in Dallas, and I wanted to see Rebecca again and determine if she was the woman God had for me. You could say that driving to Chicago via Dallas was just a bit out of the way, but it was a necessary trip that June. We had a delightful visit for three days, and I met her family for the first time. She was pleasantly surprised when on June 27, I asked her to marry me! And then, as if that wasn't enough, I added, "Do you think we can get married at the end of August?"

The reason for having the wedding so soon was that I was scheduled to teach one more year at Briercrest, and with her in Dallas, a 1,500-mile romance would have its challenges. If we were confident that God was leading us together, why not get married sooner rather than later?

OUR WEDDING

I admired Rebecca's commitment to me and my calling as a teacher and preacher. Before we married, I remember discussing whether she was indeed willing to live in Canada, far from her family, and in a climate known for its wind and snow. She insisted that she was and reminded me of the verse that became part of our vows: "Do not urge me to leave you or to return from following you. For where you go I will go, and where you lodge I will lodge. Your people shall be my people, and your God my God. Where you die I will die, and there will I be buried" (Ruth 1:16–17).

None of my family in Canada could reasonably attend our wedding, as August was harvesttime on the farm. I was thankful that my sister Ruth; her husband, Richard Anderson; and their three children were able to drive up from Mexico. I chose three of my seminary classmates to be my best men. Rebecca's bridesmaids were both of her sisters and a friend from Bible college. One of my most endearing memories was seeing Rebecca pinning pew bows along the aisles of the church just a few hours before our wedding. At the time I did not know how characteristic this was of her: hardworking, organized, taking care of things, and doing them *right*!

August 30 is always a hot summer day in Texas, so we had planned an evening wedding and reception. Not having much money, we had a simple ceremony at the Mesquite Bible Church in a suburb of Dallas and close to the Central American Mission Home where the reception was held. Rebecca had worked as a secretary for CAM for the past four years, and many of her friends had helped us with the wedding plans.

My green 1965 Buick had no air-conditioning and was packed tightly with wedding gifts and all of Rebecca's personal belongings. We were not only leaving on our honeymoon, we were on our way to Canada where I would continue teaching at Briercrest. Driving out of the Central American Mission parking lot, we tearfully waved goodbye to family and friends as we embarked on our new life together.

We had made a reservation in a downtown hotel for our wedding night, but when we arrived we were shocked to discover that they had made our reservation for the next night. They informed us that every room was taken because there was a rock concert in the area. Concerned but optimistic, we got back into our packed car and turned onto the freeway. Rebecca remembered that early on she had made a reservation at a Holiday Inn many miles north of Dallas in Denton but had forgotten to cancel it. As we drove in the darkness, we encountered a traffic jam as thousands of cars were either coming or going to the rock concert. It took us a couple of hours to reach the Holiday Inn, but we were very relieved that they were still holding a room for us. It had been a long day of preparation, packing, celebrating, saying our vows and our goodbyes. We were exhausted.

The next morning, with much anticipation, we began the long drive to Colorado. Yes, we spent our honeymoon in the mountains Rebecca loves so much! Once we arrived in Aspen, we enjoyed a few days of relaxation and fun, with treks into the mountains and visits to shops along the touristy streets. Our thoughts soon turned to Canada where I was expected in a few days to begin my third year of teaching at Briercrest. As a married couple we'd be living in the same no-frills apartment where I had lived the previous two years. If Rebecca was disappointed in it, she did not complain. She was determined to make the best of what we were given, and to enjoy being married to the young, popular professor who had returned to campus with a new wife!

Not knowing anyone, Rebecca felt like an outsider during most of that year at Briercrest. She was rather shy and retiring but made new friends, and even enjoyed the beauty and challenges of the Canadian winter. And yet, both of us felt restless, with a growing conviction that there was something beyond Briercrest that we were to do. My studies at the Chicago Summer School of Theology convinced me that I had some natural ability to understand philosophical/theological issues, and I also knew that seminaries were looking for professors who could teach apologetics (the defense of the Christian faith). I needed a PhD to qualify for such a position, so I applied to Princeton and Drew University in New Jersey. Since Drew accepted me, and Princeton did not, we felt that the will of God was being made clear.

USA, HERE WE COME

In May 1970, we packed most of our earthly possessions into the old Buick and headed to New Jersey via Chicago. There in Chicago I would spend the summer once again studying at the Summer School of Theology, then near the end of August, we'd drive to New Jersey. But we never did make it to New Jersey, because God had planned better things for us in Chicago. Again His providence led us in ways that we would understand much later. We were about to make a destiny decision.

We had little money in those hot summer days, but we were able to live in the dormitory of the University of Illinois. Rebecca had free meals in the cafeteria because she worked as secretary to the president of the school, but because I didn't work there, we had to pay for my meals. I ate very little until I received a welcome surprise: the professor who was to teach Christian Ethics had to decline, and so I was asked to teach the class since I had written a dissertation on Joseph Fletcher, a philosopher who advocated situation ethics, or moral relativism. Of course, I was delighted to do so, and since I had taught a similar course at Briercrest, I was well prepared for the challenge.

That summer I connected with some of the professors at Moody Bible Institute whom I'd known as a student in Dallas. One of them, Trevor Baird, encouraged me to stay in Chicago, study philosophy at Loyola University, and teach part-time at Moody Bible Institute. This was a new idea, but it was appealing to us because we'd already made some friends in the area, and Chicago didn't seem as far from Canada as the East Coast. The question of course was this: Would Loyola accept me into the program at such a late date? This was the end of July, and school was to begin in about two weeks.

I decided to drive to the university and discuss my situation with the dean rather than simply fill out an application and wait for a response. I made an appointment, explained my situation, and filled out an application on the spot. They evaluated it and gave me a reply a few days later. Yes, they would accept me for a PhD in philosophy, even though I'd have to take some introductory courses the first semester.

We found an apartment in the Chicago suburb of Niles and were all set, except that we needed money in order to live, pay the rent, and pay the tuition. Thankfully, through the recommendation of some new friends, Rebecca was able to find employment at the national office of Allstate Insurance Company, which wasn't too far from where we lived. Since we had only one car, I would drop her off for work in the morning, go to the university for my classes, then pick her up in the afternoon. Every dollar counted, but God was faithful in providing for us in many ways. I was asked to preach in several Chicago-area churches on Sundays, and so we appreciated the honorariums. Another blessing was that my preaching introduced us to many new friends.

WE ARE BAPTISTS NOW

A series of providential decisions led us to Edgewater Baptist Church in a northern section of Chicago, not far from the lakefront. I began as pulpit supply during the summer of 1971 while they were seeking a senior pastor. Soon, members of the congregation raised the question of whether I would be willing to become the permanent pastor. At first we said no, but the leadership was intent on pursuing the possibility and insisted that I could become the pastor and continue my studies at Loyola University. Over a period of weeks, we began to entertain the idea.

One afternoon, we met in the home of the chairman of the board to give our answer. Earlier, Rebecca and I had knelt in prayer and asked God to give us wisdom and guidance. Even as we drove to the meeting, we were not sure about what our answer to the leadership would be. As I sat there listening to the discussion, the Holy Spirit moved me to say *yes!* Rebecca didn't know what my answer was until later in the evening, but clearly, God was leading in that decision. We had recently discovered that Rebecca was pregnant with our first child, and Edgewater would provide a home and an income for us so she wouldn't have to continue working at Allstate.

One day I received a phone call from Dr. Haddon Robinson, who was my homiletics professor at Dallas Seminary. He was helping a young African American find a pulpit to preach in while visiting Chicago. Upon his recommendation, I was happy to help; and a young man by the name of Tony Evans preached a powerful message at Edgewater Baptist that morning on the topic of surrender (his text was Romans 12). Little did I know that someday this young preacher would become famous as the pastor of Oak Cliff Bible Fellowship in Dallas and be heard around the world on *The Urban Alternative*. Tony and I have met many times since then, and I like to remind him that Edgewater Baptist Church launched his preaching ministry!

MORE DESTINY DECISIONS

About two years into our pastorate at Edgewater, I received a letter from Dr. Walvoord, president of Dallas Seminary, asking if I would be willing to discuss the possibility of joining the faculty to teach theology. And, of course, I could do so while working on my doctorate at the seminary. At the same time, Dr. Charles Ryrie called and asked me the same question with the same offer. I prayed about it for about five minutes and once again with a clarity that could not be doubted, the answer was *no*. I felt no freedom to say yes to these invitations.

Unknown to me, God had The Moody Church in mind for my next destination, and so I was not free to say yes to my alma mater. Roughly five years into the pastorate at Edgewater, Rebecca and I again felt restless and believed it was time to transition to another ministry. So, when I was offered a full-time teaching position at Moody Bible Institute, we decided to leave the church and I'd restart my teaching career. I resigned in March so that I could spend the summer studying for the comprehensive PhD exam in philosophy, then I would begin teaching at Moody Bible Institute in the fall of 1977.

This was an important destiny decision, but we didn't know it at the time. Even the date of our leaving would have profound significance. The farewell at Edgewater took place on Sunday, March 27, 1977. Just one week later, a choice as to where to attend church would dramatically affect the rest of our lives.

The next Sunday, I found myself unexpectedly preaching at The Moody Church.

Gustav and Wanda Lutzer, married in 1931.

Erwin's childhood home near Colfax, Saskatchewan, Canada.

The Lutzer family c. 1947. Left to right, Wanda, Albert, Esther, Harold, Erwin, Ruth, and Gustav.

Going to school in a one-horse open sleigh.

Life on the farm provided unique preaching opportunities!

Imitating Billy Graham in high school, 1959.

Shy little Erwin on the farm.

The banner says it all . . . at age 17, preaching
John 15:16 at high school chapel.

Marrying the lovely
Rebecca Hickman in
August 1969.

Installed as senior pastor of The Moody Church, January 1980. Rebecca and Erwin with, from left, Lynn, Lori, and Lisa.

THIS DO IN REMEMBRANCE OF ME

Preaching a sermon, "Beauty from Ashes," on the Sunday after the 1986 arson fire from D. L. Moody's pulpit.

Erwin and Billy Graham at
The Moody Church in 1988.

Four senior pastors of The
Moody Church, at the
church's 125th anniversary in
1989, behind D. L. Moody's
pulpit. From left to right:
Erwin Lutzer, Alan Redpath,
George Sweeting, and
Warren Wiersbe.

Lynn, Lisa, and Lori in a garden in Beijing on a family trip to China and Hong Kong in 1984.

Christmas 1982.

Receiving the Distinguished Service Award for radio at the National Religious Broadcasters convention, 2011.

The Cove, Billy Graham's Christian conference center, 2010.

Wanda and Gustav at his 100th birthday celebration, 2002.

The Lutzer family—left to right, standing: Erwin, Esther, Harold, Ruth, and Albert. Seated: Gustav, Wanda

Erwin and his father at Gustav's 100th birthday celebration. The car in the background was brought by a friend to symbolize the first car the Lutzers ever owned.

Erwin and his mother on her 100th birthday, 2008.

With a tractor purchased by the Lutzer family in 1942, one year after Erwin's birth.

Delivering the keynote address at Promise Keepers, Phoenix, Arizona, 2002.

Spending time with Billy Graham in his home in North Carolina, 2011.

With Cliff Barrows, song
leader for Billy Graham, 2013.

Presenting Franklin Graham
with a copy of The Moody
Church 150th anniversary book
titled *Celebrating the Joy of
Changed Lives.*

The majestic Wartburg Castle where Martin Luther hid from those intending to kill him.

Standing in front of the iconic Wittenberg Door where Luther nailed his 95 Theses.

Preaching in the pulpit of the great reformer John Calvin in Geneva, Switzerland.

The room in Wartburg Castle where Martin Luther, in hiding, translated the New Testament into German.

Standing at an archeological site in the Old City of Jerusalem, 2013.

The Garden of Gethsemane.

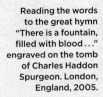

In Berlin, sitting at the desk of Dietrich Bonhoeffer, the influential German pastor and theologian executed for his role in a plot to assassinate Hitler.

Reading the words to the great hymn "There is a fountain, filled with blood..." engraved on the tomb of Charles Haddon Spurgeon. London, England, 2005.

Erwin standing between the four executive pastors who served with him at The Moody Church: Bill Bertsche, Hutz Hertzberg, Daryle Worley, Bruce Jones. (Picture taken at The Moody Church 150th anniversary dinner, May 9, 2014)

The Moody Church, Easter 2013.

3800 Seats Seat

The Moody Church, celebrating the joy of changed lives since 1869.
[Photo courtesy of The Moody Church.]

A view of the church with the original building on the left and the Christian Life Center (completed 2007) on the right.
[Photo courtesy of The Moody Church.]

Erwin, fulfilling his calling at The Moody Church.

The Lutzer family, summer 2014, Lake of the Ozarks, MO. From left to right, seated: Jack, Rebecca, Evelyn, Erwin, Isaac, and Samuel. From left to right, standing: Owen, Lynn, Shay, Emma, Lisa, Abby, Ben, Anna, Bruce, and Lori.

Erwin and daughters Lisa, Lori, and Lynn. Summer 2014.

35 years of faithful service
at The Moody Church!
[Photo taken by Dave DeJong.]

CHAPTER 7

The Providential Parking Space

᎒᎒᎒

"Erwin Lutzer! . . . I'm sick and on my way home. Will you preach for me this morning?"

Those were the words of Pastor Warren Wiersbe on April 3, 1977, as our paths crossed in the lobby on our very first visit to The Moody Church.

The previous Sunday, Edgewater Baptist Church held a farewell for us because I had resigned to devote myself to my graduate studies at Loyola University and I was slated to teach full-time at Moody Bible Institute in the fall. So that first Sunday in April, we woke up not knowing where we would attend church. I wanted to go to the "Circle Church," which was an innovative new congregation that was meeting in downtown Chicago, but Rebecca suggested that we attend The Moody Church since I had come to know Pastor Wiersbe. We had never been able to attend a service at Moody because of our responsibilities at Edgewater. As we drove on the expressway, Rebecca told me

97

how much she looked forward to sitting with me in the service, which a pastor's wife is seldom able to do.

When we arrived at Moody, there were no parking spaces, so I dropped Rebecca and our two children off at the LaSalle Street entrance and said I'd meet them in the lobby after I found a parking space. The street was filled with parked cars as far as the eye could see. But, to my delight, I noticed a man walk across the street in front of me, find his keys, and get into his car and drive away. Immediately, I backed into the space, thinking about how fortunate I was.

As agreed, Rebecca and I met in the lobby. We were surrounded by dozens of people preparing to enter the sanctuary. When we were just about to enter ourselves, Pastor Wiersbe walked past me with his coat on. He didn't see me, but I saw him, and when he brushed by I asked, "Warren, where are you going? It's only ten minutes before the service begins!" It was right then and there that he asked me to speak in the service that very morning. He'd already asked a member of his staff to repeat his Sunday school lesson for the sermon, but now that we had connected, he wanted me to preach instead.

He took the time to introduce me to one of his staff, and on the back of an envelope I quickly scribbled an outline of a message I had preached recently on Psalm 1. As I stood on the platform that morning and looked out over the large congregation, I said in my heart, "Lord, if they ever call me to be the pastor, I'll say *yes*!" Of course, I didn't seriously think that would ever happen.

But happen it did.

We never did visit another church. Immediately, people wondered who this man was who had preached on a moment's notice. Within the next week or two, I was asked to teach a Sunday school class. And a few months later when Pastor Warren Wiersbe was speaking elsewhere or on a missions trip, he asked me to preach again. When he resigned in June 1978, a committee was formed to seek his replacement. Since I was quite young and content with teaching at Moody Bible Institute, I was not immediately considered as a candidate. The elders did ask me, however, to be interim pulpit supply on those Sundays when there was no candidate in the pulpit. Since the candidates were few, I preached almost every Sunday for more than a year.

THE DIFFICULT DECISION

Even though I knew there were many men in America more qualified, I had the growing certainty that God was grooming me for this responsibility. Week by week, that conviction strengthened. But Rebecca was very hesitant and not convinced that God wanted me to become pastor of The Moody Church. During our successful five-and-a-half-year ministry at Edgewater Baptist Church, I expressed to her how weary I had become with the many details expected of a pastor. Furthermore, she felt we were too young and unqualified. This was a large church, and the thought of having to entertain everyone left her feeling exhausted and frightened. She also knew I thoroughly enjoyed teaching at the Institute. I was able to have the summers off to write and to speak in various churches on weekends, which suited my gifts and temperament.

Rebecca will tell you that she actually thought I had deceived her. She was convinced that I'd continue to be a professor, either in a Bible college or a seminary, not that we'd return to the pastorate. But the matter of The Moody Church couldn't be avoided and it began to cause tension. I respected my wife's assessment, but God had planted The Moody Church in my heart. I believed that He had specifically led us there; we simply had to accept it. I told Rebecca, "Someday I will be the pastor of The Moody Church; it is as certain as the conclusion of a geometric theorem!"

As the weeks passed, God began to change Rebecca's heart. By the time the committee extended a formal call for me to become the senior pastor in November of 1979, Rebecca chose to trust my judgment and the Lord's leading as evidenced by the support of the congregation. I began my duties on January 1, 1980, but the official installation service was held on January 20. It was one of the most beautiful winter days I can ever remember in Chicago. The sun shone brightly without a cloud in the sky. That evening I wrote these words in my diary:

> *This day marks a highlight in my life. Dr. Walvoord and Dr. Sweeting each gave a good word to us and the congregation.*
>
> *Even the weather was beautiful; the temperature was in the 40s with not one flake of snow on the ground. Lord, I am Yours for whatever You desire! Grant me grace to minister with blessing!*

I interpreted the unseasonably beautiful weather on the day of my installation as evidence that God was smiling on the occasion. We came with the goodwill of the congregation, hopeful that I would grow with the ministry, and that I'd be able to give leadership to this well-known church. I was overawed with my new role, knowing full well that I was following in the train of many great pastors and Bible teachers. My predecessor, Dr. Warren Wiersbe, was especially known for his ability to clearly expound Scripture and communicate profound truth—and for his wit. Soon I had to step into his shoes by recording *Songs in the Night* (which began broadcasting in 1943 and is the longest-running Christian radio program on air to date) and *Moody Church Hour*, which was carried on many stations. Eventually, this radio ministry would grow to include a daily radio program called *Running to Win*.

Together, Rebecca and I have learned that God's providential guidance extends to all the details of our lives—even to a parking space. *If* we hadn't decided to come to Moody that Sunday back in 1977; *if* that man hadn't pulled out of his parking spot on LaSalle Street at exactly the right moment; *if* I hadn't been standing where I was in the church lobby, I would have missed seeing Pastor Wiersbe—if any of these "ifs" and a dozen others had not happened, I might never have become the pastor of The Moody Church. As the days and months of my pastorate moved along with unexpected trials, I often consoled myself with the assurance that *I had become the pastor of The Moody Church by divine appointment.*

GRACE IN OUR MARITAL STRUGGLES

Rebecca has written about her own struggles during our early years at The Moody Church in her book, *Life-Changing Bible Verses Every Woman Should Know.* In summary, by my accepting the pastorate of The Moody Church, she felt as though she was being called to an impossible task. Back at Edgewater she had many friends—women her age and the age of her mother—who helped her adjust to the life and demands of being a pastor's wife, but now at The Moody Church, she felt alone and overwhelmed by the expectations she thought the congregation had for her.

By the mid-eighties she felt very dissatisfied with her life and began to experience a midlife crisis. She had negative thoughts about herself and earnestly sought the Lord to try to understand what was going on. God allowed her to go through many months of darkness. Since her mother's death in December 1985, she had experienced much inner turmoil, anger, dissatisfaction, and discouragement. She began to recall many horrible events from her childhood and realized that she had picked up some sinful, negative attitudes that were now affecting the children and me.

For my part, I failed as a husband. As someone who had never experienced depression (except during those dark days when I was dating Carol), I simply couldn't understand why she'd be so negative when there was so much positive happening in our lives. God had led us into the leadership of one of the best-known churches in America; we had three beautiful children and a modest but adequate house to live in; we were living the American dream, as the saying goes. Rebecca, I thought, should just pick herself up, look around, and realize that we were indeed privileged and had so much to be thankful for.

In retrospect, I realized that I was a part of the problem. I wasn't a helpful husband; I had become detached from family life as I became more involved in the work and ministry of The Moody Church. By depending so much on her to run the home (she is, by all accounts, an incredibly competent woman), I was disengaged from much of what went on in our household. Rebecca took care of our girls, did the shopping, made decisions about the house, and accomplished all this and much more with wisdom and proficiency. I later realized that "I was really not at home even when I was at home." My mind was on preparing sermons, guiding my staff, writing books, and speaking in different parts of the country. How I wish I could relive those years; how differently I would minister to Rebecca's needs through my words and actions. But the past cannot be changed, only forgiven. And forgiven it is. God was merciful to us.

Let me quote "the rest of the story" in Rebecca's own words from her book, *Life-Changing Bible Verses Every Woman Should Know*:

God began to deal severely with me, allowing me to go through many months of darkness, doubt, and soul-searching. He loved me so much that He could not allow me to continue to live with a rebellious and stubborn heart. Thus began a period of quiet despair, depression, deep loneliness, and spiritual oppression. It seemed as though God had put me on a shelf and said, "I can't use you until you surrender and are broken." I had great anguish of spirit as God broke me, and I came to the place where I acknowledged God's sovereign control over my life.

Sometimes I lay facedown on the floor as I wept and wrestled with God over my sin and the sin that had been done to me. I often read the Psalms and in brokenness asked for God's merciful forgiveness and cleansing. No one knew what I was going through, not even my husband. On Sundays it was agonizing to sit in church, hold my head up and be a kind, friendly pastor's wife. I wanted to disappear and hide; surely everyone could see my agony.

Slowly my senses returned, and God began to heal and restore. I felt like a new person and eagerly sought the Lord's will. Now once again, I asked the Lord about a dream I'd always had in my heart, "Lord, is it in Your will for me to ever become a nurse?" It was as if I heard His voice say, "Yes, now is the time, you may begin!"

Even from childhood, Rebecca had wanted to be a nurse and thought God was calling her to become a missionary nurse. But when God closed that door, her desire to become a nurse didn't leave. Now that she'd come through her depression, she had a renewed interest in fulfilling her dream. So in the late 1980s she began her studies in algebra, chemistry, microbiology, and other nursing courses.

As for me, I could see that nursing gave Rebecca a sense of her own self-worth and self-identity apart from that of being my wife. When she graduated from nursing school, I made sure that we had a great party, and I even arranged for her father to come from Texas and surprise her at the event. She then worked as a nurse for about ten years and loved caring for and comforting the sick, praying with patients and families, and holding suffering and dying people in her arms. Even though she hasn't worked in a hospital for almost fifteen years now, she continues to do some of these same things for those in our congregation who are sick or having surgery. Given Rebecca's home background, I marvel at how wonderfully God has molded her into a caring, understanding pastor's wife.

I am glad to say that we enjoy each other's company and together seek to grow old gracefully. The tension we experienced in the eighties is but a distant memory. Rebecca is a woman of prayer, a wise mother, and now, decades later, a caring, doting grandmother. Every day we affirm our love for each other and our desire to live out all the days God gives us.

Even during those dark days, I never doubted Rebecca's loyalty and love for me. And, as the next chapter demonstrates, I desperately needed her support early on in our ministry at The Moody Church. Unexpected challenges lay just around the corner without us knowing it.

CHAPTER 8

Dark Days,
Sleepless Nights

~❧~

E very new pastor comes to a church with the general goodwill of the
congregation. There were both optimism and a sense of excitement
now that The Moody Church had found its pastor for at least the next
few years. But within four months some well-wishers turned against me,
some even predicting that my time at Moody would be brief.

Early on, the elders dismissed two staff members for two different—
but important—reasons. We didn't do it as well as we should have; by
wanting to protect the reputation of both, we didn't give a complete explanation of our actions to the congregation. This sparked a backlash,
and the elders, and I especially, were severely criticized.

Certainly, during the course of my thirty-five years as senior pastor,
we've had a number of staff who have either left on their own or, have
been asked to leave for various reasons, such as their gifts not being a
good fit for what we needed. I remember having to tell one staff member that the elders felt he should begin to look elsewhere for a position
because he wasn't performing well at The Moody Church. I felt as if I

had just stabbed someone and then walked away and left him bleeding in the ditch on the side of the road.

Throughout the years, pastors have often asked me what lessons I've learned in ministry. I often reply, "I have learned that it is much easier to *hire* than to *fire*!" Because I have sometimes misjudged the abilities and character of some whom we've hired, I'm more wary during the selection process. I personally seek as much input as possible about a given individual. I've learned that staff, whether assistant pastors or support staff, can either be a blessing or a burden. One interesting fact of human nature is that I've yet to meet a staff member whom we have dismissed who felt that they deserved what was coming to them; unsurprisingly, they didn't have the same assessment of themselves as we did. To see ourselves as others see us is indeed a divine gift.

Some of our best pastoral staff have been homegrown. They're young men who have proven themselves through their work as interns, or in various volunteer capacities, and have grown with the ministry, and so they were invited to join the staff. I shall deliberately refrain from mentioning the names of any pastoral staff members, knowing that if one deserves honorable mention, then others must also be included. So I'll limit the names to only those who've served as executive pastor under my leadership: Bruce Jones, Daryle Worley, Hutz Hertzberg, and Bill Bertsche. In each case, these men were committed to the ministry and loyal to me. Never once did they seek to undermine me or manipulate people and events to their own advantage. I mention this because so many pastors tell stories of how other staff members have either tried to usurp their own authority or turn others against them. Thankfully, I have never had rebellion or insubordination among my staff. The faithfulness of these executive pastors freed me up to preach, write, and become involved in other ministries.

Though handling dismissals weren't easy, there were other, much more difficult trials waiting for me.

THE CHURCH IS BURNING!

One Wednesday, January 15, 1985, as I arrived at the church at about 8:00 a.m., I was shocked to discover it surrounded by fire trucks and police cars. When I entered the sanctuary, it was so filled with a cloud of smoke that I could scarcely see the ceiling. I quickly learned that an arsonist had broken through the door at about 6:00 a.m. and began a fire right in the platform area.

He also broke into my study and took my attaché case along with a few other items. When the police asked us who we thought it might be, we immediately mentioned a deeply troubled man who had volunteered to help in our office a few weeks earlier. On one occasion when I had counseled him prior to this, he explained that he had become an exhibitionist because it was the only way he could attract attention.

At this point I was introduced to the complexity of how "Chicago works." I gave a detailed report to the police as to what we knew about the fire and the possible suspect. Then, hours later, the arson squad came and I rehearsed the same information. In the end, there were three separate investigations: the fire department, the police, and the arson squad, but none of them communicated with the others.

The fire was headline news in Chicago, and hundreds of volunteers came from all over Chicagoland to help us get the church ready for Sunday services. The experience gave many of us firsthand exposure to "smoke damage." Every one of the nearly 3,800 seats was individually cleaned and the floors swept, sometimes multiple times. ServiceMaster showed up on their own to clean the carpets. And, although the fire was on a Wednesday, by Sunday, with the smell of smoke still in the air, we gathered together for worship and I spoke on the topic "Beauty from Ashes."

The extent of the damage was about $750,000 and thankfully, this was covered by insurance. Every one of the books in my study had to eventually be cleaned because smoke had embedded itself in every crevice of the church. The most extensive damage was to the organ pipes, which had to be dismantled, put on semitrucks, and taken to Kansas for repair and reinstallation several months later.

A DEATH THREAT

We told the police who we thought might have committed this crime. A week or two later, he surfaced, leaving a death threat for me on the church phone: "Erwin Lutzer, you will be dead within twenty-four hours!" We talked with the police, and they suggested that I, and my family, spend the next night in a motel, which we did. The police in Park Ridge, the suburb where we lived at the time, said that they would have a squad car drive by our house every once in a while during the night for the next few nights.

Then, a week or two later, the suspect showed up on a Monday evening while I was leading an Executive Committee meeting. He left a note with one of our janitors, who was asked to give it to me. The note from the arsonist stated that he was in the area. We called the police and he was arrested.

The arsonist was angry with me because when I learned that he was dating a young woman from the church, I warned her that this man was bad news, and my recommendation was that she end the relationship. In fact, if I remember correctly, I told her that she could even use me as her excuse, telling him that I was the one who counseled her to break the relationship. Thankfully, his anger was directed toward me rather than her.

After his arrest, he told us that he had taken the two flags (back then we had both an American and a Christian flag flanking the choir loft) and put one under the organ console and the other under the piano, poured a flammable substance on them, and lit them. He also prayed, "God, this is not against You . . . this is for Erwin Lutzer." The two musical instruments he lit were as old as the church building (built in 1925), so they flared up immediately. What was left was just a pile of wires and a frame where the piano stood, and in the case of the organ, a frame and metal coils, two of which I cleaned and use today as bookends in my basement library at home.

After his arrest, we had to deal with his trial. Believe me when I say that I went before four different judges to resolve his case! The first judge transferred it to another because the crime was committed in a different jurisdiction; the second transferred it because it was an arson case. I have forgotten why the third transferred it to the fourth judge, but this I can tell you: at the fourth hearing, a public defender with an empty manila folder and a piece of paper sat down to ask me what happened, and I had to tell the story right from the beginning. He told me that the files from the previous court had not arrived and we had to start over. From here on, the details are unclear to me, but eventually the arsonist was given ten months in the Cook County Jail. I visited him there and we talked through a glass window for about ten minutes.

Even though we had a restraining order against him, years later he appeared at The Moody Church at one of our concerts and greeted me, "I am the Reverend . . ." I alerted our security detail, and two of our men detained him and called the police. After the scuffle in our lobby, a boy was later asked by his father how he liked the concert. He said he didn't care much for the music but "the fight after the service was great!"

However difficult that experience was, it could not have prepared me for the one several years later. I will now tell you about my darkest days of ministry.

CHURCH DENIES ENTRY TO AIDS VICTIM

The topic of AIDS was in the headlines in the early 1980s, but by 1990 it was well established that the deadly disease could not be communicated unless there was a "transfer of fluids." Ryan White, of Kokomo, Indiana, contracted the disease through a blood transfusion and was often in the news because he was visited by Hollywood stars who made him the poster boy for the AIDS epidemic, reminding people that it was not just a "gay disease," as it was initially dubbed, but a disease anyone could get. Homosexuals who felt they were unfairly targeted made sure the story was in the news every day. As for Ryan himself, this wonderfully brave boy died a year later because of the disease.

Into this highly charged atmosphere, a couple came to The Moody Church who had adopted a child they called "Joey" who had AIDS. Some parents who had children in our Sunday school complained that they didn't want their child in the same room as Joey in case there was either a transfer of fluids (such as might happen when a child has a cold), or more ominously, if Joey were to have a cut on his arm that might be touched by another child. So, one of our staff asked the parents of Joey if they would keep their child at home until we had studied the matter further and could write up a policy that would include "universal precautions" so that we could assure other parents that their children were safe from any transfer of the disease.

Joey's parents told their story to a neighborhood newspaper, which was then picked up by the *Chicago Tribune* and other media outlets. A media firestorm erupted with calls coming into the church regarding what happened and asking how we could discriminate against this child. Initially, I did not want to talk to the press, believing that the story would soon fade. I was wrong.

Meanwhile, I woke up the next morning unable to get out of bed because of extreme dizziness, which I experienced perhaps once or twice a year (I had no recurrences for about fifteen years but had another episode in May 2013). This vertigo was so debilitating that I could scarcely move my head on the pillow, much less get out of bed. Meanwhile, my staff was calling me, telling me that the media was constantly contacting The Moody Church, and media trucks were circling the building, insisting on a comment confirming or denying the story. One of our church members who was visiting London, England, said he knew all about what was happening because he saw the story as it developed on CNN.

By noon of that day, although I wasn't completely over my serious bout with dizziness, I was stable enough to have a staff member tell the media that I'd be at the church for a press conference at 2:00 p.m. Rebecca drove me to the church, and we opened the doors a few minutes before two, which was followed by a media rush to set up all of the equipment in time for the press conference. If memory serves me correctly, about forty different media outlets were represented.

I began with an opening statement saying that Joey would be invited back to the church (in fact, we tried to contact his parents that morning so that they could join us for the news conference but were unsuccessful). And I said that if other parents had a problem with that, they could opt to keep their children at home so they would not have contact with Joey.

Of course I was bombarded with questions: Had I not heard of Ryan White? And, did the reversal of our decision have anything to do with the media exposure to the story? And, how could I as a Christian turn an innocent five-year-old away from Sunday school? And what did I think other parents would say about our decision? And more.

As if I needed further proof, I certainly got firsthand exposure to how the media can distort a story to make a person or institution look bad. The next morning all of this was the topic for the talk shows in Chicago, and one commentator put it this way: "Just imagine you are a little boy and you go to church and the pastor kneels down to have eye contact with you and he says, 'Little boy, get out of here!'"

On the next Sunday, however, the local media showed up and did a story on how Joey would now be invited back and that our doors were open to everyone. They even did some positive stories about how this could turn out for the good because other churches were facing the same issues.

Then came the hate mail. People wrote to tell us that "D. L. Moody would roll over in his grave if he knew that the church he founded wouldn't admit a little boy." Some of the mail was even vulgar, condemning us in no uncertain terms. The following week when I left the church and walked directly across LaSalle Street to go for lunch, a car rolled down its windows and someone shouted epithets at me.

When our policy was finally completed weeks later, we made it known that we would share it with whoever wanted a copy. We received at least seventy requests for it, and many churches took advantage of our work and used our policy word for word.

Yet the storm was not quite over.

ANGER, DISTORTIONS, AND FORGIVENESS

More fallout was to come. Enter Austin Miles.

Austin Miles, who had one time been an Assembly of God minister, wrote a book about how he had left the faith to join agnostics. A few years before the "Joey incident," he and I were on a popular Chicago program with Milt Rosenberg titled *Extension 720* to discuss Miles's book, *Don't Call Me Brother!* Miles argued that the atheists he met were more moral than most Christians, and he had plenty of stories he thought proved his point. On the other hand, I, of course, argued that despite the many faults of Christians, most were honorable, and I reminded the audience that "Jesus Himself didn't do anything wrong" and people should not turn away from Him just because Christians are sometimes a bad witness.

In 1990, the year of the "Joey incident," I was sent another more recent book written by Austin Miles, titled *Setting the Captives Free.* In the book, Miles again told the story of why he, as a minister in the Assemblies of God, left the church and the Christian faith. The book tells more stories of people who had had a terrible experience with their church, suffering injustice, exploitation, and so on. Miles wrote up these stories, venting his own anger toward the church and explaining why he was proud to be an agnostic.

The "Joey incident" happened just as Miles was about to complete *Setting the Captives Free.* In it, he wrote the following about The Moody Church and me:

The most outrageous example of "mocking God" that I've ever heard of came out of Chicago on April 19, 1990 . . . Rev. Erwin Lutzer, pastor of Moody Church . . . banned a little boy from attending Sunday school, where "the love of the Lord Jesus is taught" . . . Rev. Lutzer slammed the door of his Sunday school in the face of a little, dying, innocent five-year-old child! I suppose that if one is in perfect health, with money to give and doesn't ask questions but just follows instruc-tions, then Rev. Lutzer and his Moody Church (an appropriate name) is just the place to go.

Next, Miles refers to the fact that he and I had previously met on a talk show in Chicago on WGN radio, *Extension 720*, and how on the show he had made a disconcerting remark about Christians. He says that back then he felt bad for me, especially when he remarked that atheists and agnostics were more moral than Christians.

But now, he continued:

> *Now that I've learned how hardhearted Rev. Lutzer is I need no longer be concerned whether I had hurt the feelings of this bag of wind, or any other lug-headed preacher.*[1]

However, despite his vitriol, this story has a happy ending. Years later I met Miles at a National Religious Broadcasters Convention, where he was promoting a new ministry of some sort. And when I reminded him of who I was, he asked my forgiveness for what he had written. He had come back to the Lord, he said, and regretted what he had written about me, and although he was still wary of the church, he had decided to make peace with it. Of course I gladly forgave him, and our reconciliation reminded me of the power of the gospel. Yes, the gospel, once embraced, leads to a spirit of forgiveness and reconciliation.

These stories are not the only situations that kept me awake at night. Another is the court case filed against me and The Moody Church.

More trials lay ahead.

CHAPTER 9

The Lawsuit

꧁✤꧂

I was sitting in a barber's chair having my haircut when my cellphone rang in May of 2002. My administrative assistant informed me that a registered envelope had arrived at The Moody Church; upon examination, she said that we'd been served notice—a lawsuit was being filed against the church, the chairman of our elders, and me.

The elders of our church had acted to withdraw the ordination of a man who had previously served on our staff and was ordained at The Moody Church. He had left a few years before and was now the pastor of another church. Three of the leaders of his church came to us several weeks earlier, expressing their concerns about their pastor and the church in general. We had reason to believe their charges since similar stories had come to us from others who were either connected with the church or had knowledge of the situation. We wrote out the charges and sent them to four people: the pastor and the three leaders who had come to us with their concerns. We also invited the pastor to come to The Moody Church to meet with those who were bringing the accusations, but he refused. So, in April 2002, his ordination was revoked.

To be clear, we were only concerned about withdrawing the ordination that had been bestowed on this pastor by The Moody Church. We did not interfere with his church as such; if his present congregation wanted to keep their pastor, that was their decision. This is why we sent our letter only to the pastor and those who brought the charges; what these three did with the information was entirely up to them.

In July of the same year, Rebecca and I joined our sanctuary choir on a tour to England. As we visited various churches, and occasionally had the opportunity to do some sightseeing, my mind would go back to the lawsuit that was waiting for me back home. I honestly thought that once all the facts were known, the plaintiff's attorney and any judge who might be involved would clearly see that the case was without merit and it would be dismissed.

How wrong I was!

Yes, it is true that the first judge on the case dismissed the lawsuit, based on the First Amendment: namely, that the state has no right to interfere with the affairs of a church. If a church that conferred an ordination wishes to withdraw it, it has that right. But a few months later, the case was reinstated by an appellate court (a court of appeals) that tried to show that our defense was weak. Thus continued a long saga of judicial involvement that lasted for ten years and one month. Welcome to the world of courts, judges, and the law!

The case bounced around to various judges as the years went by. Our attorney (and later a second attorney retained by The Moody Church) attended the various hearings; I was content with an update, and informed about the issues that were being addressed. Eventually, one judge, who said he had listened to *Moody Church Hour*, withdrew himself from the case because he felt he could not be impartial. He handed the case to a judge who was beneath him on the totem pole (so to speak), and so the case was now under the jurisdiction of a man who was not a great supporter of the First Amendment.

BEFORE THE JURY

Incredibly, this ecclesiastical matter that should have been protected by the First Amendment eventually ended up going to civil court, and the facts of the case were tried by a jury in March 2009. For one week, various witnesses were called on one side of the case or the other, while my lovely wife, Rebecca, and I sat there with our attorneys, listening and praying. When the case finally went to the jury, we expected that they would deliberate for perhaps, at most, a few hours because it was plain to us that all the evidence was on our side. But after a day of deliberation, we received word that the jury was deadlocked. The judge, however, ordered them to come to some kind of a conclusion. Clearly, neither he nor any of us wanted to go through this ordeal again.

So it was that after six full days of court hearings, then waiting a day and a half (they deliberated for a total of thirteen hours), the jury finally reached its verdict. The judge then called us back into the courtroom and the verdict was announced: The Moody Church and the chairman of our elders were found to be innocent of all charges, but I was found guilty of putting the plaintiff in "false light"; that is, I was accused of writing a letter that contained falsehoods. And further, the plaintiff was to be awarded $267,000.

We eventually appealed this decision back to the appellate court (the same court of appeals that had reinstated the case a few years earlier). They simply ignored a mountain of case law evidence that we presented to them. Our attorney was grilled by the three-judge panel and answered the questions respectfully and with precision. The plaintiff's attorney didn't even appear, but simply sent his son to represent him.

I'm sure this young man has plenty of promise, but it was clear to us by his answers to a few softball questions, that he didn't have a grasp of the issues. But that did not matter to the judges.

Several months later, we learned that this appellate court voted to deny our appeal. The obvious bias we saw during our hearing prepared us for the verdict, though we never gave up hope that they might rule in our favor. And so, having lost that appeal, we wondered what we could do next.

Our attorneys then filed a brief with the Supreme Court of Illinois, but the court refused our request to hear the case. As you probably know, courts take only a limited number of cases, carefully choosing those that are of particular interest or significance. Apparently ours did not reach that high bar.

THE APPEAL TO THE SUPREME COURT

Our attorneys then appealed to the Supreme Court of the United States, which has a process for reviewing a case without officially hearing it. If they think the case is seriously flawed, they can remand it back to the appellate court for further review. We had good reason to believe that they'd grant us this small concession by seeing that the plaintiff's case was contrary to an overwhelming number of previous court opinions.

To be clear, we didn't expect that the Supreme Court would actually take our case since it has a crowded schedule and only reviews a small fraction of the cases submitted. But we thought that surely they would clearly see the weakness of the plaintiff's arguments and thus ask the appellate court to redo its work. Nothing is more basic than the right of a church to grant and revoke an ordination.

On Monday, June 18, 2012, we received word that the Supreme Court refused our request. After ten years and one month, we had come to the end of our legal options. We lost the case against me, and as a result, our insurance company had to pay the plaintiff his settlement of $267,000.

Through much of these ten years I was on an emotional roller coaster. One day our attorneys would optimistically predict that the case would be won, and a week later we'd hear that for one reason or another there was a continuance. As the lawsuit shifted from one judge to another, each gave hopeful signs that the case would be dismissed, then for some reason we'd find ourselves back at square one. I can't possibly remember the number of times a court date was postponed. Even after we lost in the jury trial, we were confident we would win on appeal.

I began to spend much of my Bible reading time in the Psalms. Of course, I'd read them many times before, but now I read approximately five a day, going through the entire book every month. I had never realized the number of times David requested God's help in the midst of his own trials. David frequently had his own doubts about God's care, and frequently pled with the Almighty to come to him in his distress. I read some Psalms so often that I was practically able to quote them.

Although God didn't give us the verdict we hoped and prayed for, I saw the hand of God in multiple ways, both big and small. And in retrospect, I learned a great deal about the courts, attorneys, and human nature. A wise pastor told me that when someone opposes us, we must always remember to think beyond their opposition and remember that God is working in their lives as well. In other words, we mustn't let our personal thoughts and experiences define who that person is. Ultimately, it is God who knows who we truly are, and we must leave many unresolved matters to Him.

What are the lessons I learned as a result of this ordeal?

HUMAN JUSTICE IS IMPERFECT

I felt sorry for the jury during the one-week trial. They were, I'm sure, reasonable people, chosen from the rank and file of our society. But there is no doubt they had difficulty understanding matters such as the meaning of ordination, church polity, and the separation of church and state. They were there, of course, to assess facts and not weigh in on legal issues. But all these issues were intertwined in the ensuing evidence on both sides of the question. And as one witness after another took the stand, how were they supposed to distinguish the truth from lies, and the relevant issues from those that were distracting and irrelevant?

The verdict they handed down was legally inconsistent and reflected how divided they were on the matter. The judge clearly instructed them to assess our guilt or innocence based on a single letter that contained the accusations, a letter signed by me and by the chairman of our elders. But, incredibly, I was found guilty, and the chairman, whose signature was alongside of mine on the same letter, was deemed innocent. The explanation, I think, lay in the fact that the jury was divided and hence decided to split the difference. So as a compromise of sorts, the same letter that found me guilty is the same letter that found a cosigner innocent! Be that as it may, they did what they did.

Court cases are almost always messy, fraught with vengeance, anger, and a determination to win at any cost. Decency, reason, and fairness are often cast aside in the interest of making a point or winning a favorable verdict. Right now I'm thinking of an entirely different situation where a Christian couple was given custody of a four-year-old boy and his younger brother because their mother was deemed abusive and unfit to be a mother. The mother was involved with substance abuse, had no permanent place to live, and simply displayed no ability to care for her first child. Yet she had just given birth to another child.

Though the Christian couple had been given custody of both children, the biological mother wanted custody of her four-year-old son but not her two-year-old.

Incredibly—inexplicably—the judge agreed with her request. The four-year-old was returned to his birth mother, and his brother stayed with the Christian family. So these dear Christian parents had to return the boy they had come to love as their own—they had to return him to an unfit mother, who now had a new baby by a different father and lived in an apartment with a total of seven people. The four-year-old cried incessantly as he was forcibly returned to this situation, leaving his loving home and his brother behind.

All of these situations, and tens of thousands like them, make us anxious for Christ's return when justice will finally be meted out according to truth (reality). Standing in His presence, no one will be able to tweak the facts, and justice will finally come to this sin-saturated world. We will all agree that His verdict is just.

THE NEED FOR LEGAL PROTECTION

We believe to this day that the leadership of The Moody Church acted responsibly, both from the standpoint of the Bible and the law. Our elders, along with our attorneys, acted with the highest degree of integrity and thoroughness. Yet the final decision that was left in place sets a terrible precedent for churches in the United States. During the trial, the judge essentially said this: a church has a right to revoke an ordination for whatever reason the church deems necessary, *but when such action is taken, the leadership can be found guilty of defamation of character and the "invasion of privacy."*

I fear for churches in the future that are committed to their biblical obligations of church discipline. The courts in the United States often show hostility toward churches and religious organizations. I was surprised that our First Amendment rights, which in the past have always been a guarantee of religious freedom, can now be interpreted in such a way that the Constitution offers little protection to churches. We can only guess what this means for the future.

Churches need to do all they can to protect themselves against lawsuits. Since we can no longer depend upon the First Amendment to protect our freedoms as church leaders, we must try to forestall legal action by explicitly stating our rules and regulations and doctrinal convictions in our church constitutions. Though perhaps not a final antidote to lawsuits, we can, I think, prepare ourselves to face legal challenges.

At The Moody Church, we approved a revised constitution in June 2013, which explicitly gives authority to the elders to revoke any ordination given for any reason they deem necessary. The paragraph reads, "When the Elders, as those charged by Scripture with the spiritual oversight of the Church, in their sole discretion, are of the opinion that a person previously ordained by the Church is no longer scripturally qualified for ordination, that person's ordination may be revoked with such notice, including such public notice, that the Elders in their sole discretion deem necessary to effectively revoke the previously granted public recognition." That's an attorney's way of saying: *The elders can revoke any ordination they have given at any time for any reason they deem necessary.*

When our pastoral staff and church members sign this constitution, they agree to submit to the authority of the elders regarding such matters. Our previous constitution had no provision for the revoking of an ordination since its framers would have assumed that this was an obvious right based on the First Amendment. Building in legal protections in a church's constitution is vital in today's reality.

We have also put in language we hope will protect us in the event that churches will be legally forced to perform same-sex marriages. Our constitution explicitly says that we will not rent our facilities for events that are contrary to the values and beliefs in our constitution. I predict that because of laws that legitimize same-sex marriage, churches and Christian institutions can expect a flurry of lawsuits threatening the independence of the church. Legislation is being crafted that would insist that churches that rent out their facilities must rent them to same-sex couples. Furthermore, Christian organizations will soon be required to accept same-sex couples in the workplace. And to terminate an employee who gets married to a same-sex partner will also be deemed illegal.

When freedom of religion conflicts with those who believe that same-sex marriage is a matter of civil rights, freedom of religion will be expected to surrender to the homosexual agenda. Catholic Charities discontinued their adoption agencies because they refuse, on religious grounds, to assign adoptive children to same-sex couples. A privately owned photography studio has been fined for refusing to photograph a same-sex wedding. And a Christian baker must bake a cake for a same-sex couple or be found in violation of the law.

Because we hired our own attorney who worked along with the attorney supplied by our insurance company, the lawsuit cost the church several hundreds of thousands of dollars. Churches beware: our experience is but the tip of a legal iceberg.

A LONGING FOR CHRIST'S RETURN

When being unjustly accused, I've often taken comfort in Paul's words: "But with me it is a very small thing that I should be judged by you or by any human court. In fact, I do not even judge myself. For I am not aware of anything against myself, but I am not thereby acquitted. It is the Lord who judges me. Therefore do not pronounce judgment before the time, before the Lord comes, who will bring to light the things now hidden in darkness and will disclose the purposes of the heart. Then each one will receive his commendation from God" (1 Corinthians 4:3–5).

In many ways this verse is frightening to me. To think that God will reveal the "purposes of my heart"! What a thorough judgment that will be! And yet, in the midst of it, each of us—every Christian—will receive some kind of commendation from God. At last, we will all be judged according to reality by nothing but truth: truth regarding our words, truth regarding our deeds, and truth regarding our thoughts. Truth—with the entire context of our lives taken into account.

I also believe that at the judgment seat of Christ, issues that have divided believers will finally be addressed. Parents and their estranged children; spouses who have been bitterly divorced; and matters within the church—at last justice will be done to such situations and others besides. That is why Paul says that we should never take vengeance, for that belongs to the Lord.

I fully expect that in the future judgment, our own lawsuit will be retried, but this time there will be no jury, no attorney present to tweak the facts, no false accusations, and no opportunity for redress. Just the facts, just reality will be on display. And, before that Judge we will all bow and recognize the rightness of His verdict.

No injustice will be unaddressed. In the presence of "The Supreme Court" the final verdict will endure throughout all eternity.

Forever we shall sing, "Just and true are your ways, O King of the nations!"

Lord Jesus, "even so come quickly!"

CHAPTER 10

A Light to the City, a Heart for the World

tra~

"Cities," said D. L. Moody, "are centers of influence! Water runs downhill and the highest hills in America are the great cities. If we can stir them up, we can stir the whole country."

Moody spoke more truly than he knew. In his day only 10 percent of the world's population lived in cities; today it's over 50 percent, and the urbanization of the world continues to accelerate. Cities no longer shape only their surrounding areas. Today, cities shape the world. Given the great urban population of Chicago, we must see our city as having incredible potential for the growth of the gospel well beyond its boundaries.

Ever since The Moody Church was founded in 1864, it has sought to "stir" the city of Chicago with the gospel of Jesus Christ. And in doing so, it has sought to touch the rest of the United States and the world.

We believe this message that changed so many lives during Moody's era is the one message that people need today, and it will be the one message needed for the next generation. The motto in our sanctuary says it all: "Jesus Christ the same yesterday, and today and forever."

During the racial turmoil of the sixties, many Christians left the city to live in the suburbs, and The Moody Church went through its most difficult time. I understand there were discussions as to whether the church should close its doors.

The church bounced back under the leadership of men such as Dr. George Sweeting and Dr. Warren Wiersbe, and has continued to grow in numbers and more importantly, has expanded its witness to the city.

Although the name *Moody* is well known in Christian circles around the world, the name itself is confusing to many people. Relatives of mine who live in Germany wondered what kind of a church I pastored, so they looked up the word "moody" in an English-German dictionary. They were confused when they read, "given to gloomy depression or sullen moods; ill-humored." So we always say, *Moody is our name, not our disposition!*

REFLECTIONS ON 150 YEARS OF MINISTRY

In 2014, our congregation celebrated the 150th anniversary of The Moody Church. Various committees worked hard to make the celebration meaningful, and many of our members learned about our history for the first time. In addition to videos, we produced a pictorial history of The Moody Church titled *Celebrating the Joy of Changed Lives*. And of course, we urged our people to read a biography of D. L. Moody.

When D. L. Moody, a traveling shoe salesman from Massachusetts, came to Chicago in 1856, the needs of the city's poor—especially its children—touched him. In 1858, he started a Sunday school mission just for them in the city's most impoverished area—The Sands. Within weeks, a handful of children faithfully attended Moody's Sunday school—enticed by the promise of candy, pony rides, and the life-changing power of the gospel. Two years later, over a thousand children—and their parents—came to the Sunday school each week, and when Abraham Lincoln came though Chicago en route to be inaugurated as president, he stopped by to visit and spoke briefly to the children.

Moody discovered to his chagrin that churches did not want these "rowdy urchins" to come within their doors, so he began a church of his own. With twelve charter members, the Illinois Street Church was founded in 1864. The original building was destroyed in the Great Fire of 1871 and so moved to two other locations, even changing names, before the present structure was built and dedicated in 1925 (Moody himself neither saw nor preached in the present facility). The church wasn't formally renamed "The Moody Church" until 1908, nine years after the death of D. L. Moody in 1899.

On the outside of Moody's original church building, Moody insisted that a sign be placed at the door: "Ever welcome to this house of God are strangers and the poor." The same words are still found at the entrance of The Moody Church today.

Moody was a man ahead of his time. Whether in his campaigns, or when he founded schools (a total of three), he always believed that they should be racially integrated. Even in the first graduating class of the Mount Hermon School (founded in 1879), there was racial diversity. Thirty-two nationalities and ethnicities were represented, including American Indians, Chinese, and African Americans. If the gospel is for everyone, then all those who receive the good news are members of the body of Christ and should be treated equally.

Moody took advantage of the World's Fair that came to Chicago in 1893. Tents were put up with gospel music and speakers, and almost every night, meetings were held in various churches around the city to preach the gospel to the visitors. Of the two million who attended the Fair, a good percentage of the attendees were exposed to the gospel.

Although I had known a good deal of The Moody Church's history, as I studied its origins and ministry more carefully, I was surprised at the many and varied ministries the church has had throughout its long history. Evangelism, discipleship, and outreach ministries of various kinds have always been predominant. A number of missionary agencies still in existence today were birthed at The Moody Church including: TEAM (The Evangelical Alliance Mission), begun by Frederick Franzen, a member of the church and a friend of D. L. Moody, the Sunshine Gospel Mission, and the Slavic Gospel Mission. The National Religious Broadcasters met at The Moody Church for their first constitutional convention in 1944.

Of course The Moody Church is also known for those who have preached from its pulpit: British evangelist Gypsy Smith; Billy Sunday (who, I'm told, jumped from the upper platform to the lower one without using the stairs), and John Harper, an evangelist from Scotland, who, while returning to lead a second set of meetings at the church, drowned when the *Titanic* sank in the Atlantic. In 2012, I had the privilege of speaking in the church Harper began in Glasgow, Scotland, to commemorate the one-hundreth anniversary of the tragedy. Billy Graham also preached here several times before his famed trips to Europe and Los Angeles. He also preached at the Moody Bible Institute's Founder's Week in 1951, and again at a Youth for Christ celebration in 1988. Of course, some of the previous pastors of The Moody Church, such as Drs. Harry Ironside, Alan Redpath, George Sweeting, and Warren Wiersbe are still widely remembered for their writings and influence.

OUR CHANGING IMAGE

When I came to The Moody Church back in 1980, I knew that one of my first challenges would be to build bridges to our community so that, individually and collectively, we would strengthen our witness to the city. We were eager to make sure that The Moody Church would not be seen simply as a group of fundamentalist Christians who self-righteously attend church on Sunday then take delight in judging anyone who doesn't agree with them.

We began a number of different ministries to the community. There's our monthly Moody's Business Network, a luncheon in a downtown restaurant with speakers who help connect the business community with the church. Our director of Women's Ministries began Women in the Working World, as an encouragement both to our women and those of the broader community.

We also began Branch Ministries where we partnered with different urban social ministries in our community, coming alongside them with volunteers and occasional financial support. We encouraged our members to be involved in addressing the unique problems of the inner city, including teen pregnancy, gang violence, drug addiction, AIDS, and homelessness.

Racial, economic, and cultural diversity are important values to us. We believe that a church should reflect the racial diversity of its community. Regrettably, The Moody Church has not always lived out this value. On January 24, 1962, a Chicago newspaper ran the headline: "Moody Church Acts to Admit Three Negroes." Although the Sunday school had been integrated, this decision on the part of Moody Church stirred a good deal of interest. Pastor Alan Redpath is to be commended for changing the status quo. He told the congregation, "We are interested in doing something that is right before God without stirring emotional tensions."

We are so thankful for those African Americans who attended the church during the sixties when racial tensions were at their height. They felt called by God to attend and believed that the church would change. We honor them and are thankful that those days of segregation are in the distant past. Presently our pastoral staff is racially integrated.

In keeping with our commitment to diversity, in 1993, we adopted a promise statement of just fifteen words: "The Moody Church is a trusted place where anyone can connect with God and others." According to a recent survey, on any given Sunday morning, we have people from more than seventy countries of origin worshiping with us.

The bride of Christ is multicolored, for we read that in heaven there will be people present from "every tribe and language and people and nation" (Revelation 5:9). One of the highest compliments came to me from a woman who said that she had trouble being accepted in another church because of her Middle Eastern background. She said, "At The Moody Church the color of my skin did not matter. No one even thought of that; I was just accepted." So may it ever be.

THE FOUNDING OF PARK COMMUNITY CHURCH

In 1989, we commissioned our singles pastor, Matthew Heard, and sixty of our people to begin a new church that would appeal more directly to the large singles population in our community. And thus it was that Park Community Church was born, a church that now has more members than The Moody Church. The multisite church includes campuses in a variety of city neighborhoods. We have enjoyed a partnership with its leadership for over twenty-five years and thank God for their ongoing ministry.

We have also contributed to other new churches in the city with our encouragement and financial support. We are a part of a church-planting consortium that seeks to establish new churches in strategic areas of the city. We host events that reach out to other churches, whether concerts of prayer, seminars, and the Whitefield Fellowship—an opportunity for local pastors to get together and hear various speakers on topics of interest to church ministry.

THE NEED FOR COMMUNITY

Nothing happens without leadership. How thankful I am for the elders at The Moody Church who have guided me and the staff for these many years. No pastor can stay at a church for thirty-five years unless he can count on the goodwill, prayers, and support of the elders. Our chairman, Bervin Peterson has given excellent leadership to all of us, and the continuing success of The Moody Church is largely due to his thoughtful guidance.

God be thanked, He has given us a competent and visionary pastoral and support staff that has carried on the work with ever-increasing growth and blessing. Early on, it became apparent that while two thousand people can worship together on a Sunday morning, the development of communities was necessary for discipleship and personal growth. We changed the name and focus of our adult Sunday school to ABF (Adult Bible Fellowships); these have now morphed into what we call our TMC (The Moody Church) Communities. There is not only Bible teaching, but each community is challenged to become involved in projects both inside and outside the church.

Like every church, The Moody Church has its own history and its own culture—or if you prefer, its own DNA. For example, we are known for our excellence in music and for expository preaching. Though people attend from all over the Chicagoland area on Sunday mornings, due to distance and other factors, we're constantly facing the challenge of assimilating people into various facets of ministry.

We had to ask ourselves: What methods and organizational structures work best for us? Because our membership is diverse and is scattered throughout the city and beyond, we've found small groups thrive best when they grow out of our TMC Communities. Our goal for each community is to have "a God-shaped vision, to be a Spirit-filled Community, and have a Christ-exalting mission." In these and other ways, we will always face the problem of connecting people to each other and forming community beyond the broader context of our worship services. We challenge our congregation in four areas: gathering, connecting, learning, and serving.

We stress that discipleship primarily takes place within a smaller setting where there's opportunity for accountability, involvement, and friendship. Our Equipping Ministry offers classes such as church history, apologetics, the historical development of the Bible, and the like, to help people in their walk with the Lord.

REACHING TOWARD TOMORROW

Space has been a challenge for us. Our church building, dedicated in 1925, has a beautiful, historic sanctuary designed with Byzantine architecture, but it was built with very limited educational facilities. Back in the eighties we held some of our adult Sunday school classes in nearby restaurants or other facilities we could rent. It became apparent that if we wanted to be known as a church where people could "connect with God and *others*" we desperately needed educational space along with lounge areas where people could sit down and enjoy fellowship with one another.

In 1999, we were notified that a parcel of property on the north side of the building would be coming available for purchase. This property, adjacent to a parcel that the church had purchased in 1994, would allow us the first opportunity since the 1920s to initiate a building project.

January 2000 saw the launch of a stewardship campaign called Reaching Toward Tomorrow. This was to raise funds for the costs associated with the land purchase, construction of a new addition, and much-needed renovations to the existing church building, such as replacing the eighty-year-old air handling system.

Our fund-raising had hardly begun when the parking lot across the street became available for purchase. With parking at a premium in the area, this was clearly a God-given opportunity, so our leadership stepped out in faith even though the price was steep and we had already committed to build our new Christian Life Center.

Step by step, God provided. Although there were a few major gifts given toward the project, as with the original church building, a substantial amount of the funding came from the sacrificial gifts of thousands of people who consider The Moody Church their home church. Then, as more people prayerfully gave, it became apparent that God was going to allow the building to be constructed even as we were paying for the parking lot. Looking back, it's remarkable that much of this fund-raising was done in the early 2000s, after the terrifying events of September 11, 2001, and when economic uncertainty was at its height. We are so thankful that our people stepped to the plate so that we could build this structure with minimum debt.

Our new Christian Life Center not only enables us to expand our various communities, but provides areas where people can relax and connect with one another. As such, this building is used seven days a week for various activities, and we now wonder how we managed without it.

To help our people get beyond the walls of the church, we hold various outdoor events such as a baptismal service in Lake Michigan, MoodyFest (a special music extravaganza), and a churchwide picnic. Many people from the neighborhood bring their children to our annual Summer Blast (our vacation Bible school). We also offer various camping programs for our children and youth that draw people from our church and the surrounding area. In ways big and small, we want to extend our witness, especially to those who live near us.

HOPE FOR KIDS

We are thankful for an effective and growing ministry to children within our church, but we also encourage our congregation to reach out to children beyond our walls, whether here in Chicago or other countries. Hope for Kids is part of our Global and Local Outreach program, and continues D. L. Moody's legacy of ministry to children at risk—whether orphaned, in foster care, living in poverty-stricken neighborhoods, or in danger of being trafficked. As such, we partner with seven different ministries that are committed to reaching and helping children in dark situations.

For example, As Our Own is a Christ-based, community-driven movement in India that rescues children from enslavement and sexual exploitation. Founded by Moody Church missionary Ralph Borde, this ministry, as its name implies, treats these young girls as we would want our own daughters treated. Ralph is uniquely qualified for this ministry. He was born and educated in India and came to the United States and was successful in business. Despite his business success, he felt the call of God to take responsibility for a small orphanage his father had founded. Under his leadership, the ministry has expanded, clarified its vision, and is redefining orphan care in India. These young girls are cared for and trained in responsible vocations, and the ministry gives ongoing, lifelong counsel and discipleship. Teams from The Moody Church visit India to help and encourage this growing outreach. Currently, we're raising funds for The Sparrow's Nest, a larger, newer facility for orphan care on fourteen choice acres of land.

Perhaps the most enduring ministry that's helped change our relationship with the Chicagoland community is By The Hand Club For Kids.

In the spring of 1997, Donnita Travis, a member and volunteer at the church, asked God a simple question: How do You want me to spend the rest of my life? In reply, He gave her a burden for children. In 2001, By The Hand Club For Kids was launched in The Moody Church with sixteen students from Chicago's most under-resourced and crime-ridden areas.

By The Hand invites the Chicago Public Schools principals in these tough neighborhoods to identify children who aren't meeting their reading standards, who are failing, and who are in need of critical intervention—basically, the children most likely to drop out of school. With the approval of at least one parent, the children are enrolled in this after-school program.

Bused safely to one of the four By The Hand locations, the children attend chapel where they hear the gospel, are trained in various disciplines, and are schooled in Christian living. Hundreds of volunteers, recruited from various churches, serve as tutors each week to help their designated child with homework and reading skills.

As you might expect, By The Hand has caught the attention of the Chicago School Board because of the incredible results it has in taking failing children and turning them into honor roll students. Years ago, former Mayor Daley said to Donnita, "We have no comparable program that gets the results you do."

But, By The Hand is more than a homework club or a place to hang out. It's a caring and loving place where our children's most pressing needs are met, one little thing, one child at a time—through the love of Christ.

Today, By The Hand is its own organization with an operating budget of $6 million. The elders of The Moody Church still have ultimate oversight, and hundreds of our church members volunteer as tutors or support the ministry financially. We rejoice because of what God has done through a woman who asked Him a simple question: "How do You want me to spend the rest of my life?" God surely answered that request.

Other initiatives for children have also had their start at The Moody Church. Back in 1985, four of our members began a crisis pregnancy ministry, which today is called Caris (Grace) that places equal value on the mother as well as the child. This pro-grace ministry has four locations throughout Chicagoland. Caris helps women navigate the complex emotions and circumstances that come with unplanned pregnancy by providing free, professional counseling.

We've also established an adoption fund for couples who seek to adopt children but don't have the resources to do so. The financial commitment makes welcoming orphaned children into a home cost-prohibitive for many Christian families. That's why The Moody Church partners with Lifesong for Orphans to offer financial provision for church members looking to adopt. Whether Moody Church attenders hope to adopt, or support those who do, we believe everyone in the church is called to care for orphans.

We are committed to keeping D. L. Moody's vision to reach out to children and help the poorest of the poor that they might come to faith in Christ and live productive lives for God's glory. If we will be judged by how we treat our children, the love of Christ compels us to take risks to do all we can to care for these little ones whom Jesus loves.

A HEART FOR THE WORLD

Before we raised a single dollar to build our Christian Life Center, we agreed to give 10 percent of all of the capital funds raised to special missions projects, over and above the church's missions budget. Total funds raised for Reaching Toward Tomorrow exceeded $27 million, which allowed us to freely give $2.7 million to various mission projects around the world.

With these special funds we were able to establish a missionary presence in North Africa; aid a refugee camp in Namibia where we built a church and a women's center; assist schools and seminaries in countries such as Belarus and Cuba; help plant a Polish church here in the Chicago area; help with the establishment of Living Faith Church in Cabrini Green; help educate national and Christian leaders; and collaborate with existing missionaries on special projects and personal needs.

All of this was done with funds over and above our regular missionary budget. We are thankful that The Moody Church has always had a missionary vision. Today we have roughly eighty missionaries serving in different parts of the world. And, in addition, we sponsor short-term missionary trips where many of our people become involved in the lives of others, helping our missionaries reach their personal goals.

THE MOODY CHURCH OF THE FUTURE

The problem wasn't Katrina. The problem was that the levees broke, and the result was that millions of tons of water inundated the city of New Orleans. The city was practically destroyed and nearly a thousand people died. If only the levees had been strong enough to hold back the water, New Orleans might have been able to survive this catastrophe.

Today we can see the first stirrings of storms headed our way, and the speed of the wind and the height of the waves will intensify as time moves on. The question for the church in the West, and the question for The Moody Church is: Will the levees hold?

The Bible begins in a garden but ends in a city, reminding us that the idea of the city was birthed in the mind of God. Ever since The Moody Church was founded in 1864, its task has been and continues to be *to engage this city with the gospel.*

We dare not retreat from the challenge of secularism, political correctness, and the moral and spiritual shifts that are taking place all around us. Instead, we must engage our diverse culture with our lives, voices, and Christian charity. We're not asked to choose between our love for God and our love for the city. We can do both, winsomely living true to our convictions even as they are challenged in the so-called "public square."

Much has changed since the days of D. L. Moody, but much also remains the same: human need has not changed; the power of the gospel, the authority of Scripture, and the triumph of Christ—these and other truths remain from generation to generation. The message of the gospel that changed so many lives during D. L. Moody's era is the one message people need today, and it will be the one message needed for the next generation. The verse in our sanctuary says it all: "Jesus Christ the same yesterday, and today and forever." We dare not become distracted by lesser things.

D. L. Moody prayed that God's burden for the lost would be transferred to his shoulders; he knew that without a passion for the lost, evangelism itself suffers, the church stagnates, and ministries die. Renewing this passion is the task of each generation. Methods change, special ministries are born and die, but the same Holy Spirit who has led us will lead those who come after us. God Himself provides continuity between epochs of history.

Looking ahead there are many challenges.

One challenge is to continue to celebrate racial diversity and reflect this value in our worship, our leadership, and our many ministries. God is the God of many nations, and yet we also know there is only one gospel and one Savior. We desire that people from all backgrounds come to The Moody Church, and we pray that they will thrive among us, using their unique talents, gifts, and perspectives. Our promise statement that The Moody Church is a "trusted place where anyone can connect with God and others" must continue to be an intentional priority. The Church, gathered in the name of Jesus, provides community, fellowship, and corporate worship that display God's larger vision that many tongues give praise to our Savior.

With the breakup of the family and the resulting disconnectedness of children growing up in dysfunctional families, The Moody Church has a unique opportunity to be a spiritual refuge to a hurting world. The rootlessness of our culture has created an even greater need for connecting, both individually and collectively, for fellowship, service, and prayer.

Evangelism during these days of cultural drift and skepticism will be more challenging than ever. As always, it's best accomplished by listening, building trust, and developing friendships that allow others to see the changes Christ brings about in the lives of imperfect but authentic Christians. As our nation becomes more secular, such interpersonal relationships will become even more critical in the future.

The Moody Church must continue to equip believers to engage the culture wherever they are—at work, in our neighborhoods, and in our schools. We need to equip our congregation to address these conflicts from a biblical point of view. We are called to demonstrate to the world that we belong to "an alternate kingdom . . . in which there is a complete reversal of the values of the world."[2]

We must also address the issue of the technological explosion that has occurred in the past decades, both in its positive and negative influences on the church. On the positive side, the Internet is being widely used to share the gospel all over the world, especially in those countries normally closed to a public gospel witness. In the future, The Moody Church can make even greater use of technology as we spread the gospel around the world.

However, this technology also comes with negative aspects: pornography, violence, and addiction to trivia and media-driven stimuli that hamper our Christian walk. The church must be vigilant in addressing these issues by directly confronting a culture awash in sensuality, moral impurity, and various forms of violence.

Young people must be encouraged to become involved in our secular centers of influence such as law, science, and politics. It's not necessary for us to win all these battles, but it is necessary for us to uphold our values, speak biblically to the issues of the day, and witness to the saving grace of Christ in our own lives in the marketplace of ideas. We have the responsibility of adapting our ministries to the changing needs of our culture.

We must be better prepared than ever to welcome dialogue with skeptics and people from other religions because, as has been said, "the mission fields of the world are now at our doorstep." Along with secularism, Islam will challenge the church in the United States on many different levels, but we must both expect and welcome such conflict, and rejoice that we have the privilege of representing Christ in times of uncertainty and opposition.

A glance over two thousand years of church history reminds us that it has often elicited hostility from the cultural, political, and religious powers of its time. Yet the church triumphed. We can expect similar challenges in the future; thus, equipping believers to share the gospel in this diverse culture is more important than ever. Church members will have to be challenged, not simply to attend church, but to *be* the church.

Come what may, we must strive to be credible witnesses to the saving power of Christ. We need to take the words of Jesus seriously: "In the world you will have tribulation. But take heart; I have overcome the world." Our assurance in Christ's eventual triumph remains our motivation to face the uncertain days ahead. The Moody Church must seek to develop Christians who are loving but tough-minded, wise but courageous, compassionate but deeply committed.

The church is to be in the world as a ship is in the ocean, but as we know, when the ocean seeps into the ship, the ship begins to sink and can't rescue others. The church has the delicate task of both engaging the world and yet being free from its sinful desires and values.

The church of the future may indeed discover there is a higher cost to faithfulness than what we ourselves have had to pay. Like the church in every generation, The Moody Church will have to prove again that "if God is for us, who can be against us?" (Romans 8:31). Only with great faith and sacrifice will the levees hold as the moral and spiritual storms challenge our resolve.

We must constantly enlarge our vision for Chicago so that, with God's help and renewed passion, The Moody Church will remain *a light to the city with a heart for the world.*

"He who calls you is faithful; he will surely do it."

CHAPTER 11

Integrity, Witnessing, and the Green Pickle Award

❧

There is a story about a beggar who met Saint Francis of Assisi and asked him, "Art thou St. Francis?"

"Yes."

"Then take heed that thou *be as good as men believe thee to be*!"

That story comes to mind because as pastors we know that our people believe we are "good" not just in public but in our private lives as well. And we should be "as good as the congregation believes we are." None of us lives up to such a high bar, and yet God's standard of integrity has not changed.

Almost every morning before I get out of bed I pray, "Father, glorify Yourself in my life at my expense." I want to begin each day with the basic perspective that it's not about me; it's all about *Him*. At the end of the day, what is most important is that God is glorified. I begin each day reading a chapter of the Bible and then giving my day to God.

As for my personal prayer time, as I've grown older I spend more time enjoying God's presence than I did when I was younger. Rather than a long list of requests, I spend time giving God my heart, quoting praises and requests from the Scriptures. I become quiet before God, letting Him search my heart, and invariably, there is sin that needs to be confessed or issues of surrender that the Holy Spirit brings to my attention.

Recently, I met a woman whose mother was an incredible woman of prayer, and although her husband was mean to her and even carried on affairs, she stayed with the marriage because, as her daughter put it, "My mother thrived on God." In her journals, this mother wrote that she was out of resources, and out of everything, but she was determined to cleave to God. Although my circumstances are very different, I also want to learn to "thrive on God." I'm convinced that God is more interested in who we are in His presence than He is about what we do for Him.

Though I consistently pray for my daughters and sons-in-law, it wasn't until God blessed Rebecca and me with eight lovely and lively grandchildren that I gave up on the idea of simply listing their names before God and asking Him to "bless" them. What I've chosen to do instead is pray for each one of them one day a week beginning from the eldest to the youngest (I pray for two on Saturday). And each week I choose a passage of Scripture to pray on their behalf. In other words, I frequently use the same passage for each child but adapt it to their needs and ages.

If you were in our home after breakfast, you'd see Rebecca sitting in her favorite chair with a cup of coffee, having her devotional time, reading her Bible, and praying. She prays for me, for our children and grandchildren, for her siblings, and for her friends and missionaries. She has modeled for all of us not just a belief in prayer but a steadfast faith that also enables her to cope with migraine headaches and other physical challenges. She prays for me before I preach, and often continues to pray while I preach. In fact, I often think that although I'm the one up front, we're really doing this together.

Rebecca and I have struggled with our "family devotions," that is, having a family prayer time. The problem was that, given the location of The Moody Church, I would leave the house early in the morning and sometimes stay at the church for an evening meeting. Yes, we read the Bible and prayed together, but we did so inconsistently. Our best times with the children were when we talked and prayed with them as we put them to bed at night. Currently, Rebecca and I enjoy a time of sharing and prayer after breakfast on those mornings when I am home.

The two of us also enjoy doing ministry together. Recently, we spoke at a series of Pastors and Wives conferences in Maine where I shared with the pastors and she shared with the wives. Whether we are traveling together or apart, we directly support each other with our prayers and encouragement. The books she has written have already blessed many, and I expect that her ministry will continue to expand in the years to come.

AVOIDING PITFALLS

Those of us in public ministry often receive a great deal of affirmation. People tell us about the blessing we have been, either in our writings, messages, or counseling. As a pastor, I've tried to put these comments in proper perspective. Knowing my own struggle with pride and also keenly aware of my sins and weakness, I often breathe a prayer of gratitude that I've been a blessing to others; I haven't yet lost the wonder that God would use me to help people on their spiritual journey. I think it was A. W. Tozer who reminded us that the donkey who carried

Jesus down the Mount of Olives knew that the shouting and palm branches on his path were not for him but for the Person on his back!

I have always prayed that God would enable me to rejoice over those who are more successful than I in the ministry. There are many evangelical pastors who are much better known and have larger ministries than I've had. I pray for them, encourage them, and remind myself of these words of Paul that I memorized years ago. After warning the Corinthians about becoming "puffed up," he adds, "For who sees anything different in you? What do you have that you did not receive? If then you received it, why do you boast as if you did not receive it?" (1 Corinthians 4:7). The prayer of John the Baptist has often been mine: "He must increase, but I must decrease."

I've found it very freeing to remember that the church isn't mine, it belongs to Jesus; the people do not exist to serve me; they are not there as a platform for me to showcase my gifts. These are God's people, the sheep of His pasture, and if I can have a small part in their growth and development, I shall be satisfied.

Recently I was visiting with a megachurch pastor and I said, "God is doing a great work here . . . don't mess it up!" I said it rather lightheartedly, but I meant it. Just a few weeks earlier, a very well-known megachurch pastor had to resign because he was discovered to be involved in an affair. It would be impossible for me to count the number of pastors I have known—good and godly pastors—who have fallen into the sin of immorality.

Knowing the complete devastation such a fall would be, in recent years, I've frequently asked God for His special mercy. I've asked that He would cut my life short rather than let me be unfaithful to my wife. Better to die of cancer or heart disease than to bring disgrace to my wife, my family, and the wider body of Christ.

Back in the mid-nineties, the night after we hooked up our computer to America Online, God gave me a horrific demonic dream. In my dream, three demonic spirits were trying to pin me against a wall, and the only way I could be free was to invoke the name of Jesus. When I awoke, I was shaken by this frightful experience. I knew immediately that this was a gift of God—God was, in effect, saying, "You now have in your home something that Satan will use to try to destroy you." What a warning that we all need safeguards to keep us from the availability of pornography.

The possibilities of "messing up" a ministry are endless. And may I never say that couldn't happen to me or any other pastor. Let us be warned: "Be sober-minded; be watchful. Your adversary the devil prowls around like a roaring lion, seeking someone to devour" (1 Peter 5:8).

What have I learned after years of ministry? We must certainly guard our character as our most important possession. Too often we hear of moral failure among evangelicals, and these leaders seldom regain the trust that's so important for future ministry. Like a vase shattered on the floor, it's difficult to put everything back to how it once was. And, if we are leaders, we should be worthy to be followed.

Second, my friend and fellow pastor Crawford Loritts likes to remind all of us that our power is not in our gifts but in the Giver of those gifts; we don't lead with our gifts, we lead with godliness. Christ first calls us to intimacy with Himself and then we are called into ministry. Greatness is not recognition, it is faithfulness with what God has given us. God has His ways of reminding us that it's not about us; it's about His Son.

THE NEED FOR SHEPHERDING AND PRAYER

Back in 1983, Eugene Peterson wrote an article in which he empha-sized that pastors must never see themselves as someone who "runs a church" but rather as someone who shepherds people and takes care of souls. He stressed that the work that a pastor does during the week is really no different than what he does on Sundays. On Sundays, we proclaim the gospel, but during the week, through interaction, discussion, and visitation, we must be about the same business of seeing God at work and applying His grace to our own lives and the lives of others. People look to us for guidance, for wisdom, and for the kind of pastoral care that has the best interests of our flock in mind.

At the same time, pastors also stand in need of grace and the assurance that we are not alone in the battles of life. About twenty years ago I chose about a dozen men at The Moody Church to be my prayer partners. For many years we met together the last Saturday of the month for special prayer; we prayed for each other, and then as I knelt, they laid hands on me, praying earnestly for me. I regret to say that in the past few years we have met very infrequently, mostly because of conflicts in my schedule. But they continue to pray for me, and the captain of this prayer ministry, Earl Bowers, has prayed for me nearly every day for twenty years. One of my many regrets is that I did not cultivate this prayer ministry with more consistency. To younger pastors I would say, *Gather godly men around you and let them carry you along with their consistent prayers and friendship.*

How thankful I am for the many people in various places who pray for me regularly! Among my many prayer warriors are my predecessor, Dr. Warren Wiersbe, and his wife, Betty, who assure me of their prayers; and there are hundreds of other people I have met who have told me they pray for me regularly.

At The Moody Church we have a day of prayer and fasting three times each year. We encourage people to fast on a specified Wednesday, then come to church that evening for a time of corporate prayer and "calling on God" for our families, our church, our community, and the world. And, yes, we still have prayer meetings every Wednesday evening, and although the numbers, proportionately speaking, are small, those who do come are intercessors who believe things will be different because we prayed.

AN INTRODUCTION TO REVIVAL

Early on in our Edgewater days, we made a trip back to Canada for Christmas in 1971 and discovered that there was a revival taking place; hundreds of congregations were experiencing deep repentance, and lives were being transformed. Broken marriages were being put back together, children were being restored to their parents, and Christians were willing to pay any price to be fully right with God. Store managers were surprised at the number of people who were returning to confess they had stolen merchandise; and the government was receiving back taxes from cheaters. Christians who had never told anyone about their faith in Christ were now freely witnessing to the power of the gospel.

The revival began under the ministry of twins Ralph and Lou Sutera, who discovered that revival comes not just by preaching but by giving people an opportunity to personally share their stories of repentance and transformation. Through such direct exposure to changed lives, people become convicted of their sins then go into a prayer room to seek God until they deal with whatever sins the Holy Spirit brings to their attention.

Rebecca and I were exposed to this revival fervor during our visit when a former high school teacher of mine had us over and asked me pointedly if I was taking credit for what God was doing through me. When I confessed that I was sure I wrestled with pride, he asked us to kneel at his coffee table and repent.

Although I haven't personally seen a similar revival in the United States, this experience in Canada many years ago has stayed with me. What I learned was this: sin has to be confronted directly, and being fully right with God has to be a priority no matter the personal cost. This has affected my counseling and preaching.

The revival in Canada only lasted about a year, but its effects were evident in the changed lives it left behind. Yes, some Christians reverted back to their former lifestyle, but those who daily followed through with their commitments were permanently changed. Some entered full-time Christian work.

Life Action, a ministry in Michigan, fosters revival through its many teams that hold meetings in churches. In 2010, The Moody Church invited them for a Thirst Conference, which was very well received, and their ministry revived the hearts of many of our people. Life Action also has a website, OneCry, which has recruited tens of thousands of people to pray for our churches and our nation.

More recently, here in Chicago, I have helped promote citywide prayer meetings that are held all too infrequently. But God is at work here, unifying the evangelical churches and giving us a sense of oneness in mission. I've never given up the hope that a widespread revival might still be seen in our day.

BUGHOUSE SQUARE

Whether in my private life or public ministry, I have often witnessed to others to help them on their spiritual journey. Most interesting are the people I have met randomly in a store, in the neighborhood, in a taxicab, or on a plane. Frequently, I have, in one way or another, challenged them with the gospel.

I have become friends with Illinois' most famous atheist, Rob Sherman. He and I have connected a number of times, and one day I took him out for lunch and later brought him over to see The Moody Church. As we talked, I realized that his atheism did not seem to be rooted in rigorous scientific or rational considerations, but rather in his own personal struggles in the home in which he grew up. In 2011, I debated him for two hours in a forum sponsored by our college ministry at The Moody Church (if you wish to go online, you can see and hear it on YouTube).

My philosophy of witnessing can be simply stated: it is to make Jesus look good, whether through just a random encounter or a longer friendship. At the end of the day, what people need most is to see that Jesus is a Savior worth knowing. My greatest desire is to defend the uniqueness of Christ over against other options. We have a Savior; other religions do not.

In the heart of Chicago, just south of the Newberry Library, is Washington Park, known also as "Bughouse Square." For the past seven or eight summers, I have been invited to participate in what are called Soapbox Debates, where the speaker is given a microphone and stands on a soapbox to speak on some controversial issue. Each year, I have chosen to defend the uniqueness of Jesus. For example, one year my topic was, "Why every honest historian should believe in the physical resurrection of Jesus." Another year it was, "Why Jesus has the right to be called God." Heckling and opposition from the crowd is both permissible and expected. I've accepted this invitation because it is my one opportunity each year to join Paul on "Mars Hill" where skeptics encounter the gospel.

In 2014, my topic was "The supremacy of Jesus—why He alone is able to bring us into the presence of God." As expected, there were the usual heckling and opposition, but to my surprise, at the end of the afternoon I was the winner of the Green Pickle Award, which is given to the speaker who, in the opinion of the judges, gave the best speech and dealt acceptably with the hecklers. The green pickle is a hollow plastic "pickle" about four feet long and a foot in diameter; it originated with a Dill Pickle Club that used to meet around the corner from Bughouse Square to continue the discussion of various issues.

I mention this because sharing the gospel reflects my heart; God has given me a passion to defend the gospel, giving people reasons for the superiority of Jesus over against all other options. In 1993, I spent the better part of the week at the Parliament of World Religions, which met in the Palmer House in downtown Chicago. I engaged with an assorted number of people from various religions and traditions. One evening I had dinner with a group of New Agers, and when I explained the gospel to them, they said in effect, "We have never heard that before." I wish I could say that people came to faith in Christ as a result of my witness, but I have often believed that in such contexts, my role is to point people in the right direction, not necessarily to take them all the way to their destination. We have to trust the Holy Spirit to carry them through all the way to salvation.

A COMMUNIST AND HIS BIBLE

In 1984, my family had the privilege of visiting the People's Republic of China to interact with Bishop Ding, the head of the Three Self Movement, which is the official government-approved church in China. We had the honor of spending several days with him, talking to him about the state of the church in China, the level of freedom, and the sensitive question of the house churches that meet underground (those who meet in homes and seek to survive under the radar of government surveillance). We did not know whether this bishop was a Christian or a Communist, but we did know that he was trying to do his best to walk the fine line of helping the government-approved churches and, at the same time, keeping within the good graces of the Communist governmental authorities.

152

Though I've forgotten much of what he said, I shall never forget this comment: "I know who you as evangelicals are, and if you traveled the length and breadth of China you would discover many people who believe just like you do. Persecution has wiped out all theological liberals in China; only the evangelical faith has survived."

"Of course!" I thought to myself. "Why would a liberal who does not believe that Jesus is the Son of God or the only way to the heavenly Father—why would he be willing to die for a purely human Jesus?" After walking on the Great Wall of China and seeing a few other sights, we flew home, and on the flight I was again reminded that God guides our steps even when we are unaware of it.

En route from China back to the United States, we had a four-hour flight from Hong Kong to Tokyo but were unable to sit together as a family. I found myself sitting next to a well-dressed Chinese man, and I'm ashamed to say that I did not initially begin a conversation with him, assuming he did not speak English. I was minding my own business reading the book of Luke, but when there were about thirty minutes left on the flight, we struck up a conversation. I was gratified to discover that he could speak at least some English, and so I began to explain the gospel to him. I asked him if he had ever seen a Bible before seeing mine.

"Oh no, I have never seen a Bible." He told me that he was an atheist, a professor of chemistry at a university in Beijing. "If only I could give this man a Chinese Bible!" I thought.

Our daughter Lori, who was sitting directly ahead of me, overheard my remark and said, "Dad, Mom took that Chinese Bible from our hotel room in Hong Kong, and she has it with her." I couldn't believe this; why would Rebecca take a Chinese Bible from a hotel room and put it in her carry-on bag? Why didn't she tell me she was doing this? She was sitting a few rows ahead of us, and so I went and asked her if indeed she had the Bible with her; yes, she did. It was a Gideon New Testament with English on one page and Chinese on the other. When I gave it to the man he said, "So this is a Bible!" I said, "Yes, this is a Bible!" He asked me two more times: "So *this* is a Bible!" and I said yes.

He continued, "The reason I'm so interested in the Bible is because my mother was a Christian who died when I was six years old, and I always wondered what Christians believed."

The big jet was beginning its descent into the Tokyo airport, so now I excitedly shared the gospel with him, complete with an Evangelism Explosion diagram. Then I said, "I have no doubt that God planned that I would be next to you on this flight. Your mother probably prayed that someday you would be with her in heaven, and God arranged it so that you would hear this good news and believe on Christ to join her someday." The man smiled. When I said goodbye I told him, "I want to see you in heaven, and your mother is waiting for you too!" He smiled for a second time and said, "Well, who knows?"

I am confident that that man will be in heaven; I believe that with a copy of the New Testament in Chinese, he soon devoured its contents and believed the gospel. Since then I've often spoken at Gideon conventions, and when I tell this story, they tease me about my wife "stealing" one of their New Testaments from a hotel room in Hong Kong! But Rebecca, bless her, didn't steal it, for on it was written, "You may take this copy of the New Testament." She couldn't say why she took it; she just did it on impulse. Who can doubt that she was led directly by God to take that copy of the New Testament and put it in her carry-on bag because there was a chemist whose mother's prayers needed to be answered?

GOD OPENS DOORS, WE WALK THROUGH

I attempt to witness to many people I meet, though I don't feel obligat-
ed to do so unless God opens a door—and He does so with a great deal
of regularity. For example, on a plane after an exchange of pleasantries,
I'll ask a question such as, "Where are you on your spiritual journey?"
Then I just listen, asking helpful questions along the way. Unless we
find out where people are on their spiritual pilgrimage, we can't speak
to their specific need. I don't have a set method; I simply respond to the
situation as it presents itself. Sometimes I just throw out a hint to see if
people will pick up on it. I'll say things like, "God bless you" or, "Has
God been blessing your life lately?" By their reaction I can tell if they
are open or closed to spiritual matters. I try to have books or booklets
with me that explain the gospel, and I leave these with people, telling
them why its message is so important. I've found that if we're looking
for opportunities and are open to the Spirit's leading, sometimes within a matter of minutes, we'll be discussing the gospel.

On a plane, an older woman from a liberal church said to me, "One
thing I know for sure, there is no hell." I quizzed her on how she could
know this, because after all, we cannot observe where the soul goes after death; she must have inside knowledge about what exists and what
does not exist in the invisible world. When she admitted that what she
said was just her personal opinion, I, smiling to make the truth easier
to grasp, said to her, "You have put me into a dilemma . . . you say there
is no hell, but Jesus spoke about hell often, at least as many times as He
spoke about heaven. Obviously, there is a conflict here, but I do think
that Jesus knows a great deal more about these things than the rest of
us. So, I don't want to hurt your feelings, but I'm going with Jesus on
these matters!"

Of special importance is our ability to witness to Muslims, many

155

of whom drive taxicabs in Chicago. After I introduce myself to them as a "Christ follower" (the word *Christian* carries so much baggage for them), I introduce the topic of Jesus Christ. They explain that they regard Him as a prophet, but I help them see that He is much more; He is both a Mediator and a Savior. God has supplied Him for us, and He is the only One who is able to forgive our sins and take us to heaven. When they object to the Trinity, I point out that we believe in a spiritual trinity, not a physical one, therefore it's not contradictory to believe that there are three persons but one essence.

Then comes the challenge: I go on to tell them that there are things mentioned in the Bible about Jesus that are not in the Qur'an, which if a Muslim were to believe, he could go to heaven. At that point, the Muslims I've encountered are both appreciative and curious, waiting to find out what those two facts might be.

The facts are that (1) Jesus died on the cross for our sins; and (2) He rose from the dead and then ascended into heaven. I explain why it is necessary to accept Him as Savior since He alone can bring us to God.

I don't argue, but I do defend the uniqueness of Jesus, saying that He was not just a prophet but actually a Savior who can take away our sins. And if we want to be reconciled to a holy God, we need Someone qualified to bring us together—Someone who is as great as God Himself. Thus Jesus, who was born of a virgin and without sin, is uniquely qualified to be our Savior and Mediator.

In this context, I do not get involved in a detailed discussion of the Trinity or question the character of Muhammad. I have one objective, and that is to keep the focus on Jesus as a Savior and a Mediator. I also at times have given a brief testimony of what Jesus has done for me.

Most important: leave the driver with a copy of the gospel of John and tell him to read these stories about Jesus. Nearly everyone to whom I have left a copy of John's gospel has received it with appreciation. I see my duty as simply doing what I can to open his heart to the beauty of Jesus. For those who live next door to Muslims, friendship and love is the key to building those bridges into their hearts and helping them to see beyond the stereotypes as to who Christians are and who Jesus is.

Surely there's never been a time in the United States when there are as many opportunities to reach out to our Muslim neighbors as today. Did not Jesus tell us we would be witnesses to all nations? Those nations are now at our doorstep, brought here by God to hear the wonderful message. Let's not bypass these God-given opportunities. We represent Christ in every context in which we find ourselves.

Perhaps one of the most encouraging compliments I've received is from a man who was seated at a table next to me in Elly's Restaurant across the street from The Moody Church. After greeting him, we talked about a variety of things. I discovered that he was a retired doctor whose specialty was tropical diseases. I mentioned to him that my sister had been a missionary nurse in Africa for thirty years and had encountered such challenges among the people, and that she herself had to be treated for malaria. He was very interested, and we continued to talk until the conversation drifted to his granddaughter, who had by now joined him at his table.

Finally, he asked me, "What do you do?" When I told him I was the pastor of The Moody Church, he could scarcely believe it. He said he never expected that the pastor of The Moody Church would be so open and accessible. He ended by saying, "If you are the pastor, I might actually come to your church sometime."

I'm not sure exactly what this man expected the pastor of The Moody Church to be like, but I suppose he did not expect him to be friendly, open, and in general, a pleasant dinner partner. How tragic that we have so often not made Jesus look attractive in a world that desperately needs to know that there is a Savior who can bring us into the very presence of God.

As the Father sent Jesus into a needy world, so we are sent to represent Jesus in a world that needs hope. Whether in public or private, we are privileged to be His representatives.

CHAPTER 12

Lessons My Children Taught Me

❧

I n the summer of 1971, Rebecca and I were relaxing at Ravinia, a music park outside of Chicago, listening to Strauss and Mendels- sohn, when I found my mind wandering, contemplating what it would be like to be a father. Just a few weeks earlier, we had learned that Re- becca was pregnant and would give birth to our first baby the following March. In those days, of course, we had to wait until the child was born to know whether it was a boy or a girl.

Often we as parents think of all that we've taught our children, but I've come to realize that I've learned a lot from my children, so I thought I'd share a few of the lessons our children taught us over the years. After all, raising children enrolls us in a new curriculum char- acterized by never-ending patience, forgiveness, and endless wonder.

We made many mistakes when we reared our children: inconsistency in discipline, favoritism, and lack of consistency in family devotions, to name a few. But apparently we did do some things right. When our oldest daughter, Lori, was asked why she tells her friends that she had good parents, she says that we were willing to admit when we were wrong and ask forgiveness as necessary, and that what we said in public we lived out in private. She'll also say that we prayed for them regularly and told them so, and that we loved them unconditionally.

Rebecca enjoyed being a mother; she was determined not to repeat the mistakes and abusive behavior of her parents. She worked hard to give our children a happy and fun childhood, filling our home with music, books, birthday parties, friends, a passion to know and love God, and many opportunities to learn and experience wonderful things. She often sacrificed doing what she wanted to do in order to help our girls with homework and projects, and drive them to the many activities they were involved in. Rebecca now loves being a doting, caring, helpful grandmother. All parents enroll in a curriculum, and the teachers are our children and grandchildren.

Here are some lessons they taught us.

FIRSTBORN STRONG-WILLED CHILDREN CAN BE A BLESSING

Lori was a precocious child who challenged our judgments about life in general and our rules in particular. It seemed that our firstborn entered the world asking theological questions and pursuing justice for everyone. She loved dollhouse miniatures, animals, music, and reading. She also loved to use her verbal skills to share her opinions with anyone within earshot. We knew little about parenting, and now with a strong-willed child, our knowledge and patience were challenged. Rebecca and I came from differing family backgrounds, and we had to develop our own parenting techniques to apply our theories in real life. After her youngest sister, Lisa, was born, Lori was told that her own birth was difficult because of the circumference of her head, to which she characteristically replied, "I couldn't help it because those were my brains!"

Being a firstborn, Lori always received a great deal of attention and love, but in junior high and high school she struggled with a sense of insecurity. In spite of this, however, she had many friends and showed leadership, organizational, and teaching abilities when playing with her sisters. We strove to keep her challenged academically, and made sure she always had plenty of good books on hand. She loved the travel adventures we shared as a family, including trips to Europe, the Middle East, and China.

Her theological inquisitiveness produced questions like these: "Who was taking care of the world when Jesus was a baby?" and "Did Jesus know I was going to fall off my bike?" When she was five, I remember praying with her as she "accepted Christ as her Savior," but we could only wait to see whether this decision was real or not. To the glory of God, her profession of faith would prove to be genuine, even when severely tested.

When it came time for her to go to college, she chose Indiana University—a secular school—where we knew she would "sink or swim" in the unsympathetic environment. As it turned out, it was a good choice. When her Christian faith was challenged or ridiculed, she, ever the one to take an opposing position on various issues, chose to defend her faith. She attended a good church, took part in a Navigators Bible Study, and during the Christmas season of her first year, called me to say, "Dad, you can go to sleep tonight and know that your firstborn has made Jesus Christ the Lord of her life!"

And yes, I did sleep well that night, knowing that our oldest daughter had made Christ the Lord of her life. In many respects, I think we failed her as parents for not understanding her creative nature and inhibiting her self-confidence. Years later she told us that with our frequent discipline, she felt condemned, as if she were either unworthy or basically a "bad girl." But despite our many failures as parents, God had worked in her life and brought her not just to saving faith but also to become a woman whose light would shine even in dark times. I've often had to ask her forgiveness for my inconsistent discipline or anger, rather than being a sensitive and patient father.

During her junior year at IU, she met a tall, handsome young man named Bruce Bourne, who was a student at Asbury University in Wilmore, Kentucky. His parents lived in Bloomington, Indiana, and one weekend on a visit home, he showed up at the Navigators Bible Study that Lori attended. They were married on June 4, 1994.

A couple of years later, Lori and Bruce experienced the loss and sorrow of delivering a stillborn daughter whom they named Sarah—our first grandchild. Our hearts were broken as we held our precious granddaughter in our arms, reminding us that life is filled with both joys and sorrows. We believe very deeply that this little one whom we did not get to know on Earth will be with us for eternity, and even now "beholds the face of her Father in heaven."

Lori and Bruce have blessed us with two more grandchildren, both of whom she homeschools. Rebecca and I are amused that "the apple doesn't fall far from the tree," as Samuel and Anna are bright, precocious, and sometimes challenging—just like their mother. Lori is trained as a Montessori teacher and has a successful website where she sells the beautiful teaching materials she's developed at montessoriforeveryone.com.

Lori's lessons to us: If you have a strong-willed child, don't let their behavior cause you to overreact, to lose your cool, or to retaliate in anger. Your consistency in discipline and self-control will pay off if you're patient. Don't overestimate the extent to which you can influence your child; ultimately, the child must be given to God for transformation. Only God can convert a child and capture their heart; don't try to push them into making a decision for Christ. God gives us children to raise for His glory and He's always there to help us along the way.

Pray. Pray. Pray.

SECOND-BORN, COMPLIANT CHILDREN HAVE STRUGGLES

Lynn, our second child, had a tender heart, a sensitive spirit, and was anxious to please us and others. She was the peacemaker who tried to avoid conflict and either willingly or unwillingly would surrender her rights for the sake of peace and calm. She was our compliant child and didn't challenge our authority. Lynn was our social butterfly, a popular, teenager who loved her friends, and her friends loved her. She took some leadership positions in high school and became a talented cheerleader, and she also loved to sing and dance. There were many occasions for her to witness to her friends, and help them work through their problems.

Lynn had a number of boyfriends along the way, usually nice, decent guys, but not necessarily Christians. I recall her crying for days when one of them broke up with her. When I tried to assure her that God had kept her from a bad decision, she refused to be comforted. She learned that when you love someone, you risk having your heart broken. Rebecca offered her wisdom that was empathetic yet realistic: "Lynn, it's possible to love the wrong person." Her feelings were powerful, and she'd learn more lessons of the heart as time went on.

When her next relationship was headed in the wrong direction, Lynn wrestled again with her feelings and sought me for support and direction. I remember a specific conversation that took place in her bedroom as she poured out her confusion and fears to me. I put a pillow under my head and lay on the floor and listened without criticism or judgment as we had a long talk. She was able to share her heart and her misgivings and gain courage to end the relationship. Teenagers need a father to talk to when going through the turbulence of romance and its implications. Yet I also failed her. My times of listening and giving her attention were all too few. When she was in her first year of college, she gave me a letter that was like an arrow to my heart. She felt (correctly) that I had often been too busy to spend time with her, especially when she needed me emotionally. She wrote, "I feel like a book on your bookshelf. You take me down occasionally and flip through the pages and then put me back on the shelf. And I can't compete with Martin Luther and all the other books in your study!" To think that I had put my academic and ministerial interests above that of my daughter was a wake-up call. How insensitive we parents can be, even when we're serving the Lord.

Our city girl and socialite believed that God wanted her to attend Taylor University, nestled among the cornfields of Indiana and far from the big city. Once there, she settled down and became a serious student, made some great friends, and completed her undergrad in three years. It was also there that she seriously dated a fine young man who was a growing Christian. But after dating for two years, he wasn't ready to commit to a permanent relationship and their romance ended. Lynn was devastated and returned heartbroken to live at home as she sought God's will for her life.

She began a master's program in counseling at Trinity Evangelical Divinity School, and as she studied, it became clear that God wanted her to prepare her mind and heart to help others through a counseling ministry. During her second year, she began dating a handsome seminary student from Missouri named Shay Roush. This time it was for keeps, and on December 27, 1997, they were married. Since July 2002, they've been ministering together at the Crossing in Columbia, Missouri—Shay as a pastor and Lynn as a part-time counselor. She's gained much insight into both the Bible and human nature, often taking upon herself the many burdens of others. She's learned to apply biblical wisdom to the deeper issues of the heart, and her life experiences, including heartache, have powerfully shaped her ability to speak grace and truth into people's lives.

Lynn and Shay have blessed us with three grandchildren: Jack, a sports enthusiast and athlete; Emma, a creative and intuitive social butterfly; and Owen, the "brainiac" who is a piano prodigy and future engineer.

Lynn taught us that teenagers need parents who maintain an open, nonjudgmental relationship, which is the key to guiding their hearts. And when their hearts are broken, they need our acceptance, love, an offer of hope for their future, and the assurance that God knows best and that, in His time, He'll bring the right person into their lives.

LAST-BORN CHILDREN CAN BE STRONG AND RESILIENT

Lisa, our last-born, was a charmer with a sweet, sensitive spirit. She's the one who, at perhaps the age of four, said at bedtime, "My teddy bear knows he isn't real!" From her earliest days, she had fun with her sisters, and loved to bake and spend time in the kitchen with her mother. Like her two sisters, she had natural musical talent and took piano lessons for many years. In high school, she enjoyed singing and acting on stage, performing leading roles in shows like *The King and I* and *Guys and Dolls*. She was exceptionally gifted in math, which became evident in grade school. She continued to excel in high school and eventually graduated from Wheaton College with a degree in physics and secondary education. She also enjoyed studying German and had the opportunity to spend a summer in Germany during her college years, learning the language and experiencing the culture.

In a chemistry class at Wheaton she met a bright, handsome young man named Ben Dykstra from the Chicago area. After a three-year courtship they were married on May 20, 2000. God's allowed them to walk through several trials, especially relating to Ben's career. Their story is a testimony to the providence of God's timing and protection.

Ben was in the ROTC program at Wheaton College at a time when the United States was at peace throughout the world, so he and his classmates didn't anticipate being deployed to a war zone in the foreseeable future. But the world changed when our country was attacked on its own soil by militant Islamists on September 11, 2001.

Ben's first assignment with the army was to Baumholder, Germany, in February 2002. This put him in the European theater, from which thousands of troops would be sent to fight in Iraq. During their three years there, Ben and Lisa were very involved in the Protestant Chapel on Post and the Hospitality House, a ministry by Cadence International to the US military. Fourteen months into this assignment, Ben was deployed.

A FATHER IS BURIED ON THE DAY
HIS GRANDDAUGHTER IS BORN

In March 2003, the Iraqi War began with the first wave of US troops. Ben was included in the second wave of troops that came from the 1st Armored Division in Germany. So Ben and Lisa tearfully said goodbye and he walked into the darkness along with hundreds of other soldiers to board vehicles that would take them to an airport to fly to Kuwait. From there they would form a vast army of tanks and Humvees to cross the desert and enter Baghdad.

To her great surprise, within a week's time Lisa discovered that she was one month pregnant with their first child. Her joy was overshadowed by the knowledge that she faced her whole pregnancy alone without Ben by her side, not knowing if he'd be able to be with her for the birth of their baby. God had yet another challenge for this young couple that would run simultaneously with the deployment and pregnancy, and would bring sorrow and loss.

During the month of June, Ben's formerly healthy father, David, was diagnosed with terminal lung cancer. The doctor was up front about his prognosis, giving him six to nine months to live. Thanks to many prayers, Ben was allowed to leave Iraq and fly home to spend a couple of weeks with his ailing father. By now Lisa was on an extended visit with us in Chicago, so she and Ben were a comfort to his family in their sadness and uncertainty.

The time passed quickly, and Ben soon returned to his responsibilities as a signal officer living in one of Saddam Hussein's palaces in Baghdad. Meanwhile, David's cancer worsened, and Ben was often in dangerous situations. When Lisa returned to Germany in July, she began to experience deep loneliness, fear, and depression. After much prayer and family discussion, she returned to Chicago to live with us and await the birth of her baby.

By early December, Ben's father David could no longer walk or speak, and it was clear that the end was getting near. Lisa was conflicted, longing for Ben to be with her for the birth of their baby, but knowing that it was even more important for him to be with his family at his dad's passing and funeral.

Which would come first, David's death or the baby's birth? On several occasions, Rebecca and I knelt with Lisa at our living room couch, praying that God would somehow work these events out for His glory, helping Lisa and Ben to accept whatever God's plan would be.

By the middle of December, David entered hospice with only a few days to live. A Red Cross message was sent to Iraq, informing Ben's unit of his father's imminent passing, which permitted Ben to leave immediately. He arrived in Chicago on December 24, greeted at the airport by Lisa, who was eight-and-a-half months pregnant.

Ben's father died on December 30, in the presence of his entire family. The funeral was planned to take place on January 3, 2004. But one more surprise awaited Ben and Lisa—and all of us.

As God would have it, we awoke on the morning of the funeral to discover that Lisa was in labor! Ben and I drove to the funeral, where I was honored to lead the service and Ben was able to give a tribute to his father's life. Meanwhile, Rebecca and Lisa drove to the hospital.

Immediately after the funeral and burial, Ben came to the hospital and was present for the birth of their daughter, Abigail Rebecca. "Abigail" means "father's joy," and she certainly brought joy to our entire family on that day, a day of tears and joy. Ben's mother, Samara, newly widowed, joined to share the joy with grandmother Rebecca and the rest of us. As Samara held Abigail, she rightly said, "You are a special baby, for you have brought so much joy to us on this day of sorrow."

God had answered our prayers and graciously allowed Ben to be present both for his father's death and for his daughter's birth. Although we never would have dreamed that these events would culminate on the same day, God had it planned long before! God answered Lisa's question, "why now?" that she'd asked so many months before in her lonely apartment.

Ben returned to Iraq on January 16, 2004, and continued to serve there until July, when he was reunited with Lisa and baby Abby in Baumholder, Germany. Two years later, he was deployed to Afghanistan, after which he left the army to find a civilian job. Since May 2007, they've lived near Indianapolis, and now, Abby has a sister, Evelyn, and a brother, Isaac. Ben works for Pepper Construction as a quality manager, and Lisa is a devoted stay-at-home mom, keeping family life and schedules going strong. The sorrows of the past are still remembered, but their focus is the joy that comes to those who keep trusting God even when they don't understand His ways.

Lisa taught us how to walk alongside our children when the difficulties and trials of life overwhelm them. Their struggles become our struggles. We learned that parenting our children is a calling that will be our heritage until we die. And when the grandchildren enter our lives, we have the privilege and responsibility of leaving them an important legacy.

CHILDREN AND GRANDCHILDREN, OUR LEGACY

Our grandchildren give us insights about God, human nature, and ourselves as we watch and listen to what they say and do.

Our oldest grandchild, Jack, taught me a lesson about how we sometimes have a wrong view of God. When he was about four years old, we were playing hide-and-seek in the backyard. The idea was that he was to run behind some trees and I would try to find him. But to my surprise—and grandfatherly delight—he simply stood under a tree and covered his eyes with his hands. He must have thought that if he can't see me, I must not be able to see him! I immediately thought to myself, there's a sermon illustration here: because we can't see God, we often think He must not be able to see us; but there's no place for us to hide from His all-seeing eyes. In His presence we can only hide in plain sight.

Our children and grandchildren test our theology by asking us unexpected, difficult questions. Such as the one Abby asked as her mother was talking to her about God. "Is God bigger than heaven, or does He just make Himself fit?" Then eight-year-old Owen asked his mother, "What is more complex to understand, the Trinity or infinity?" I'd say both are rather hard to understand!

When our granddaughter Emma was about five or six and afraid of the dark, her mother said to her, "We will pray that God will be with

169

you in the dark." Emma responded, "No I don't want to pray. I don't want God in my room all night!"

Sometimes our children make comments that encourage us. Anna, upon hearing that there will be rewards in heaven for serving Jesus, said with a great deal of seriousness, "I think Papa will have lots of rewards in heaven because he tells so many people about Jesus!" Thanks, Anna, I needed that!

Evelyn was about four years old when we were celebrating the birthday of her older sister. She must have felt neglected because she went into my study, closed the door, and began to sing, "Happy birthday to *me*! Happy birthday to *me*!" A reminder that if we don't bless our children with attention, they will get it even if it is from themselves!

As for three-year-old Isaac, he reminded us that it is later than we thought it was when he said, "Mommy, it's thirty o'clock!"

When our grandson, Samuel, was around five years old, I took him for a walk in a forest preserve, complete with hidden trails and a winding river. As we turned on a path to return home, he said, "No, Papa, this is the wrong way. We have to go home over here!" pointing to a path that led in essentially the opposite direction. "No, Samuel, this is the path. You have to trust me," I said with confidence. Reluctantly, he walked toward me kicking the dirt with the stub of his shoes. "But Papa, it is so *hard* to trust!"

Yes, it is hard to trust. We were standing in a forest preserve where I'd walked for years; I not only knew the trail we were on, but I could already see the roof of our condo through the treetops. I also knew that the trail Samuel wanted us to take would lead away from the condo all the way to the Des Plaines River. He reluctantly trusted me, and it paid off. In a few moments we were home.

That made me think of how Jesus knows exactly where we are on our journey; He knows where all the paths that appear before us will eventually lead and He knows the enemies, snares, and trials that are waiting for us along the way. And yet, my grandson Samuel was right. *It is so hard to trust!*

But like Samuel who laid aside his doubts and followed me, just so we must trust Jesus who will lead us all the way home. And, we pray that we will bring our children with us.

Recently our entire family was together for a few days of fun and fellowship in a retreat atmosphere, a vacation we look forward to every summer. Our three daughters always sang together when they were growing up, their voices coming together in a perfect blend. At our last gathering, they beautifully sang praises to God and I remarked, "If I were to die today, I would die satisfied knowing that my daughters and their spouses love God and that our eight grandchildren are being raised for God's glory."

There is no greater joy than to see children walking in truth.

THE WIDER FAMILY

When we came to Chicago back in 1970, we were befriended by a couple in the small church we attended; Dick and Jan often had us over for dinner, they let us babysit their children, and one day, they stocked our fridge with food. They knew that young couples don't have much money, and such friendships and gifts are appreciated. Also, an older couple, Harry and Ruth Verpleogh, took us under their wing and treated us as if we were their own children. They introduced us to their friends, invited us to eat out with them, and even helped us financially. These families were models to us of kindness and generosity, which we have in turn often shown to younger, needy couples.

Several years ago, God brought a family into our lives who needed emotional and spiritual support. When I was speaking at a Bible conference at Camp of the Woods in Speculator, New York, I met a couple with four children. One day as we ate lunch together, the wife, Beth, told me the story of how she had suffered various kinds of abuse by her devious parents. Years later, when she and her husband confronted her parents about the wrongs they had done while she was growing up, they denied it and rejected her. As she began to weep, I said rather spontaneously, "Well, if your father has rejected you, I'll adopt you as my daughter!" Little did I know that these words spoken without forethought would eventually lead to a wonderful relationship between Jeff and Beth Paine and their four children, Lauren, Michael, Nathan, and Katherine.

This new relationship provided an opportunity for Rebecca and me to informally "adopt" this family and enjoy the responsibility of being surrogate grandparents. Because they live in Texas, we see each other only about once a year, but we're in contact often and exchange birthday and Christmas gifts. Best of all, we pray for each other, and this younger couple can look to us for advice and emotional support. The Paine family is a wonderful example of raising good and godly kids. They've expressed their love and appreciation to us many times, how thankful they are that God brought us into their lives. Through their friendship and prayers we also have been blessed.

The bottom line for all of us is that in this broken world, we all can connect with people beyond our immediate family. It is unchristian for us to build a comfortable wall around ourselves when we have the privilege of being the hands and feet of Jesus. The promise of Isaiah is that if we give ourselves to the needs of those around us, we in turn will be blessed: "Then shall your light break forth like the dawn, and your healing shall spring up speedily; your righteousness shall go before you; the glory of the LORD shall be your rearguard" (Isaiah 58:8).

In a day when families are crumbling for any number of reasons, it's more critical than ever that we invest time, resources, and above all, our affection for the members of our family and for the wider body of Christ.

God is our Father and we are His representatives here on Earth. May God grant us the grace and endurance to raise children for His glory and honor.

CHAPTER 13

People along Life's Way

I've had the good fortune of having mentors who've guided and encouraged me on my journey from my early days to my latter years. Ever since my pastor back in Bible college told me to connect my two short messages and make them into a respectable Sunday evening sermon, I've had people who believed that I had the gift of ministry and gave me the confidence that I could both preach and be a leader.

If I could redo my ministry, I'd spend more time discipling men, helping them with their leadership in their homes and teaching them the need for moral purity and mutual accountability. When I transition from the leadership of The Moody Church, it's my desire to spend however many years God gives me to mentor young pastors, giving them the encouragement that others gave on my own journey.

Some men have been my mentors without knowing it. I've met and benefited from the friendship of many evangelical leaders. Even before I became the pastor of The Moody Church, I frequently connected with James Vernon McGee both formally at meetings and personally at lunches or breakfast. Though he passed away many years ago, he's still heard on hundreds of stations with his *Through the Bible* program.

Most people might not know that he had a great sense of humor. When he was given an award at the National Religious Broadcasters Convention, he began, "I believe in two natures—the old nature and the new nature—when I was told I was to come here to get this award, the new nature said, 'Don't do it, you don't deserve it'—but the old nature said, *'Go and get it!'* and so here I am!"

Billy Graham was on the dais waiting to speak as McGee continued, "I believe that in heaven, God will reward every Christian, whether they have lived fully for Christ or lagged behind. Why, *I believe even Billy Graham will get a reward!"* As for Billy, he laughed along with the rest of us.

As a pastor, it's rewarding to be able to discuss matters of ministry with people who aren't necessarily members of your own church or staff. As I mentioned earlier, David Jeremiah and Joe Stowell were classmates at Dallas Seminary. I've spoken for and connected with John MacArthur of Grace Church, and have been personal friends with four presidents of Moody Bible Institute: Drs. George Sweeting, Joe Stowell, Michael Easley, and Paul Nyquist. These friendships have enriched me immeasurably. My own predecessor, Dr. Warren Wiersbe, has been a confidant and prays for us regularly. I've been humbled to speak at the Brooklyn Tabernacle in New York and observe firsthand the powerful prayer ministry of pastor Jim Cymbala. I cherish our friendship. I've also benefited from ministry friendships with men such as Charles Colson, Ravi Zacharias, James Dobson, Tony Evans, and John Ankerberg. Rebecca and I have enjoyed friendship with female leaders such as Kay Arthur, Nancy Leigh DeMoss, and Carol Kent.

For several years, eight or nine of us Chicagoland pastors met four times a year to get better acquainted and discuss ministry matters. In the mix were men such as Bill Hybels, James Meeks, James McDonald, and Wilfredo DeJesus, so you can imagine how lively and challenging our discussions always were. These friendships helped strengthen our own witness to our communities. But most of all, I've been greatly blessed by the pastoral staff members of The Moody Church, with whom I have had a sense of unity in mission, in fellowship, and mutual support.

About ten years ago, I had lunch with Francis Cardinal George, who retired last year after long and faithful service. He's a kind man, highly respected in Chicago and the nation; he's often sought out by the Vatican on matters of church leadership and policy. In our respectful two-hour discussion it became painfully clear that "the Reformation is not over" as some allege. The cardinal is very committed to traditional Catholic doctrines about the sacraments, the role of Mary, and the like.

After lunch at his residence, I gave him a tour of The Moody Church. He asked why there were no statues, no relics, and not even a cross within the church. I explained that this represented our theology: that God works directly in our hearts in response to saving faith and that there's no need for images; indeed, these might actually detract from our confidence in the very promises and presence of God. Our visit was cordial and respectful, but it also clearly revealed our differences. I continue to pray for the cardinal as he battles the cancer that has forced him to retire.

On twelve occasions over a period of about four years, it was my privilege to speak at large Promise Keeper rallies. What a privilege to speak to tens of thousands of men in St. Louis or Minneapolis–St. Paul on issues such as forgiveness or sexual purity. But one of the events especially stands out in my mind. When I arrived at the stadium in Phoenix, the leadership took me aside and said, "The evangelist who was to give the opening sermon tonight isn't here because his plane was delayed. You are going to give the evangelistic sermon tonight."

Secretly, I was elated. I had always wanted to preach that first night when an evangelistic sermon was given, and I'd come prepared for a moment just like this. God gave me great liberty and when I gave the invitation, hundreds of men streamed forward filling the front of the platform and the aisles. I phoned Rebecca that evening and said, "If my plane should go down on the way to Chicago tomorrow, just know I have died a satisfied man." Then I told her about preaching the gospel the opening night with hundreds of men coming forward.

AND NOW, BILLY GRAHAM

In 1988, Youth for Christ celebrated its fiftieth anniversary with an event held at The Moody Church. And given Billy Graham's early involvement and leadership of the fledgling movement back in the forties and fifties, he was the featured speaker. How gratified I was that he came to the church early so that we could spend some time together in my study. Finally, my boyhood dream had come to pass; he was the man I had admired for so many years.

Billy sat on a couch in my study and put one leg up on my desk. He'd been bitten by a spider and was in pain from the injections he received for the venom. Rebecca and I had just returned from a visit to the Soviet Union, so we discussed the state of the church in Russia. And then I told him how I had read about him as a boy, listened to *The Hour of Decision* as often as I could, and I even organized a prayer meeting in my high school for his 1957 crusade in Madison Square Garden. I ended with, "You will never know how much you have meant to me."

His reply startled me. "That's too bad . . . nobody should ever follow me. I'm such an unworthy servant of Jesus Christ, I can't live a day without Him; nobody should ever follow me." This wasn't a show; he meant what he said. The conversation drifted to other things, and then when it was time to go he asked me to pray for him. "Oh yes, I'll pray for you," I said. He replied, "I mean right now I want you to pray for me." He stood up and walked toward me, and I lifted him in prayer to God.

His humility was truly disarming; if a stranger who had never heard of Billy Graham had been looking on, he would never have dreamed that this man had preached face-to-face to millions of people, and year after year, was consistently listed among the top ten men most honored in the United States. I realized that here before me was an ordinary man whom God chose to use in extraordinary ways.

Many years later in 2011, while I was teaching at the Billy Graham Cove in Asheville, North Carolina, the Grahams' oldest daughter Gigi, knowing of my affection for her father, said that she'd take Rebecca and me to see him, though by that time he was confined to a wheelchair. So we rode in her SUV all the way up the mountainside near Montreat, to the rustic Graham home that we'd seen so often in pictures or on television. After a few minutes in the house, Dr. Graham was wheeled to a table in the kitchen, and we sat and chatted for about twenty minutes. He spoke about a book he was writing; his memory was clear about the past. When I remarked that I had helped organize a prayer meeting in my high school in 1956 for his New York Crusade, he quickly corrected it and said, "That was 1957." He spoke about his wife, Ruth, and how much he missed her since her death several years earlier.

We ended our time holding hands in prayer then said goodbye. Again I was struck with his humility. Here was a man who, for more than sixty years, was constantly recognized, photographed, praised, frequently criticized, but always pursued by the media. All that was now gone as he sat in silence and was cared for by several nurses. Yet it was clear that he was content with Christ's presence, praying for the continued ministry of the Billy Graham Evangelistic Association and its present leadership.

There will never be another Billy Graham. Not only because God loves originality, but because we live in a different age in which there's a distrust of religious figures. Though God can do anything, it's inconceivable to me that a man would be raised up to preach the gospel to full stadiums around the world. If the world is to be won for Christ, it will be through the church, with all Christians representing Christ wherever God has placed them.

CLIFF BARROWS

As a boy I also admired Cliff Barrows, not just because he was able to lead music so effectively in the Billy Graham crusades, but also because he was a close personal friend of Billy's. In 2013, Cliff invited me to speak at the Cove for his Seniors Celebration. We spent a delightful two days together with him and his lovely wife, Anne. I was both surprised and gratified to learn that they awaken at 4:00 a.m. every morning to take some medication, and then they listen to *Running to Win*. For years they were supporters of The Moody Church's media ministry.

I tell these stories to illustrate that there are times when God allows our childhood dreams to come true. Riding my father's tractor on the farm and memorizing sermons given by Billy Graham, I could never have dreamed that someday I'd meet him and be able to personally express my thanks to him for the impact he had on my life. Or, to meet Cliff Barrows, the man I admired for his warmth, obvious musical gifts, and approachable personality.

I look back with profound thankfulness for the road I've traveled. But the older I get, the more I wonder why God chose me to have the privileges that have come my way. I'm encouraged when I remember that "we have this treasure in earthen vessels, that the excellency of the power may be of God, and not of us" (KJV).

We are, it is said, the product of the books we read and the people we meet. In both of these ways, I have been blessed.

CHAPTER 14

Books, Radio, and Internet

❧

"Lutzer, how many books have you written?"

The man who was sitting across the table from me was Elmer Towns, my friend and professor back in the days when I was a student at the Winnipeg Bible College. It was 1971 and he was, at the time, a professor just outside of Chicago at Trinity Evangelical Divinity School. We were having lunch together soon after Rebecca and I moved to the Chicago area. He was the one who had written that letter of recommendation to Dallas Seminary for me eight years earlier.

The fact that Elmer called me by my last name was to my mind a sign of affection, another hint that he considered me one of his promising students. Now he was staring at me with a twinkle in his deep brown eyes as he asked me pointedly how many books I had written.

"None," I said, quite confident that my short reply should satisfy him. I had graduated from seminary about four years prior and had not thought seriously about writing a book. That was a job for professionals who had something to say.

"Lutzer, you are *lazy*, just plain *lazy* . . ." he continued.

I meekly told him that I'd written an article for *Eternity* magazine that had been accepted and would probably be published in a few months. He wasn't satisfied. He challenged me to take writing seriously and shared how he sometimes dictated the gist of an article while driving his car, then sat and wrote the article later. He'd just written a book on growing Sunday schools that had already sold out its first printing. He loved to think big and help others to think big along with him.

A few years later, Elmer left Trinity Seminary, and during the past thirty years has been dean at Liberty University, serving with the late Jerry Falwell. We've met several times throughout the years, and I reminded him of our conversation. I assured him that "Lazy Lutzer" had indeed written quite a few books. As proof, I dedicated one to him. And in 2010, he invited me to speak in the chapel at Liberty. Rebecca and I toured the school and were quite amazed at its size, its diverse options for learning, and its many thousands of students. In June of 2014, he preached at The Moody Church and we reminisced about the past and talked about the future.

Even after that lunch back in 1971 with him, I never thought I'd ever write a book. Dozens of books on every topic imaginable were available in Christian bookstores. What was left to be said? Furthermore, I had a mental block about such a project. I imagined that there were all kinds of exasperating requirements for formatting, footnotes, and matters of organization that could only be done by professionals. However, I do recall very distinctly that one snowy winter day back in Bible college in Winnipeg I said to myself that someday I would write a gospel tract!

Through an unexpected stroke of divine providence, I was finally motivated to write a book. What seemed to be an interesting coincidence again proved to be the unmistakable imprint of God's leading.

Eventually, I would write many books, but only after God connected a series of dots that led to my first published manuscript.

THE WRITING OF BOOKS

Just a few months after my lunch with Elmer, I found myself taking a course at Trinity Seminary (now known as Trinity International University) taught by John Warwick Montgomery, a man known as an authority on apologetics (the defense of the Christian faith). I was delighted that I could sign up for one of his classes even though I'd begun attending Loyola University. The course at Trinity met only once a week so it didn't conflict with my schedule.

Montgomery was an interesting professor who enjoyed making references to obscure but relevant historical occurrences. He also enjoyed debating those who differed with him, such as humanists and other kinds of heretics. One day he told us that he was scheduled to debate Joseph Fletcher, the author of *Situation Ethics*, the very book that was the topic of my thesis when I attended summer school in Chicago. So after class, I accompanied him to his office and told him what I had written. He asked if I could bring the manuscript to the seminary the next day because his debate was scheduled in California that weekend. Of course I was happy to make a special trip to give him a copy before his departure.

Montgomery read what I had written while on the plane en route from Chicago to California for the debate. That evening he quoted me in the debate, and months later when the account of the debate was published, there was a quote from me with a footnote on page 86! Given my high regard for Dr. Montgomery, I felt honored indeed.

But when Montgomery returned to class the next week, he told us about the debate and asked, "Erwin, where are you seated?" I raised my hand, and he continued, "You have demolished *Situation Ethics*; what you have written deserves to be published." You can imagine my shock and delight that I'd be commended by this man known throughout the land as a brilliant apologist. The idea that what I had written could be turned into a book had never crossed my mind.

I took the manuscript to Moody Press (now Moody Publishers), and the editors agreed that it had material worthy of publication, but it would have to be rewritten to make it more relevant and accessible to the average reader. I spent the better part of the summer reworking the manuscript, writing it all out by hand (I didn't type in those days and of course there were no word processors). Rebecca deciphered my handwriting and typed it, doing the best she could to read my scrawl.

Ten months later, my first book, *The Morality Gap*, came off the press. By then the fad of situation ethics was diminishing, so the book went through only two printings. The philosopher Gordon Clark wrote the foreword, and John Montgomery wrote a commendation for the back cover. I felt as if I now "belonged" in the world of scholarship.

I've told this story to give glory to God who has faithfully led me even when I was unaware of it. Once again, I think of the many divine providences that led to my writing career. *If* I hadn't attended summer school in Chicago, I would not have written a dissertation on situation ethics; *if* I hadn't taken a class from Dr. Montgomery, I would not have been encouraged to get it published. No wonder I feel as if I've walked through revolving doors even without knowing that I was providentially being led by God.

I've discovered that it is exhilarating to craft a document that others just might read. Although the first seven or eight of my books were written by hand and typed by Rebecca, I did eventually learn to use a computer and word processor, without which I can scarcely write a single line today!

HITLER, THE GERMAN CHURCH, AND THE
RELIGION OF ISLAM

In the early 1990s, I began leading tours to the sites of the Reformation in Europe. During one tour in 1996, I had an extra day in Berlin,
and, with the help of a boy on a bicycle, I found the courtyard where
Colonel Claus von Stauffenberg was ruthlessly killed for plotting the
assassination of Adolf Hitler (if you saw the movie *Valkyrie*, then you
know the story). The building that surrounds the courtyard contains
a museum honoring the Resistance (those who were involved in the
plot to kill Hitler). I was amazed at the details of their plans. They had
hundreds of brave people in place to take over the leadership of the
government, believing that the assassination plans would be successful.
It was also in this building that Hitler first revealed his plans to exter-
minate the Jews.

While I was perusing the displays, I saw pictures of the Nazi swas-
tika with the cross of Christ in the center. These swastikas adorned the
German churches, both Catholic and Protestant, showing their support of Hitler's Reich. As I stood there, seeing concrete evidence that
the church was on board with Hitler's agenda, I said to myself that
someone should write a book on how and why the church was seduced
by Hitler's promise of a great Germany. After I left the museum, I
caught a cab to the Kaiser Wilhelm Church where I saw the reliefs of
the German Kaiser (Latin *Caesar*) leading the people in a procession
toward Christ. The German church had lost the gospel of Christ and
substituted a nationalistic version of Christianity in its place.

That fall of 1994 I began outlining the book, and in October, I co-
incidentally happened to tell an editor of Moody Press about my inten-
tions. He quickly reminded me that April of the next year (only seven
months away) was the fiftieth anniversary of the end of Hitler's Third
Reich. He asked if I could write the book within the next three months

and then they'd put it on a "fast track" so that it would be available in April to coincide with the publicity that the anniversary would generate. I gasped but said that if God helped me, it was "doable."

Hitler's Cross was published and in bookstores in April 1995. Later it received the Gold Medallion award at the Christian Booksellers Association meeting in Los Angeles. The book was written in three months, simply because the material almost quite literally fell into my hands. I providentially came across relevant articles, talked to friends who knew important sources, and quickly found the needed research books. Since it was published in time for the fiftieth anniversary, it rode on a wave of publicity. There were so many "providences" along the way that I wrote them up in much greater detail in my journal. I can confidently say that it was God who put that book together.

My most important book was released by Harvest House in February 2013—*The Cross in the Shadow of the Crescent: An Informed Response to Islam's War with Christianity.* This book would never have come to be if, in 2009, I hadn't been invited to join a cruise to Turkey sponsored by my alma mater, Dallas Seminary. When I saw that there were no visible churches in the seven cities to which Jesus wrote letters (as recorded in the book of Revelation), I had to face the question of how Islam had been able to destroy Christianity. When a devout Muslim guide told me that Islam's ability to crush the church is proof of its superiority, I was deeply disturbed because it made Jesus look weak. I asked God for wisdom to uncover the lessons that these now nonexistent churches of Revelation had to say to the church in the United States.

This book on Islam is a prophetic book in the sense that it forecasts dark days ahead for the West because of the growing worldwide rise of a militant form of Islam. And nations, including Canada and the United States, are submitting to Islam in all of its demands. Perhaps the best depiction of this was a caption I saw on a sign near Detroit,

Michigan, where Muslims were demonstrating. It read simply, "We will use the freedoms of the Constitution to destroy the Constitution."

Because many of my books have been translated into various languages, I feel as if I have made friends all over the world. My book *One Minute After You Die* has been translated into many different languages and has sold well over a half million copies around the globe. When I traveled to Japan back in 1992, I was surprised at how many people knew about my writings. Then in 2004, I spoke at a meeting of about four hundred people in Germany, sponsored by the publishing company that has translated about fifteen of my books into German, and again I met people who knew my books.

God has chosen to weave a tapestry, and my life is a small part in His design. Blessed are those who never forget that it is He who works all things according to His good will and pleasure. I say with John the Baptist, "He must increase, but I must decrease."

RADIO BLESSINGS

In 1926, The Moody Church almost certainly was the first church in the United States to broadcast its morning service live over radio. Moody Bible Institute has also been a leader in radio technology and expansion.

When I came to The Moody Church, I inherited two radio programs: *Songs in the Night*, started by Billy Graham in 1943, and *Moody Church Hour*, which was the church's Sunday morning service edited for broadcast over perhaps a hundred stations. I felt very privileged to be the speaker on these broadcasts, following in the very capable steps of Dr. Wiersbe. I found it a particular challenge to read the transcripts for *Songs in the Night* in a conversational style, but as time went on, I became more relaxed and more able to develop a relational style.

In 1994, we began to discuss the possibility of beginning a daily radio program, so of course, we needed a title for it. I was having a discussion with our producer, Dave McCallister, about it in my office, when Hebrews 12:1 came to mind. We batted around various possibilities until I suggested we call it *Running to Win*. The name was just what we wanted: short, easily remembered, and signifying action. *Running to Win* made its debut in May 1995.

In 2006, the church became part of a joint project with Radio Vocea Evangheliei in Romania to broadcast translations of my sermons on *Alege astazi* (Choose Today). Two years later, in 2008, by popular demand, *Running to Win* was expanded in many markets from a fifteen-minute program to a twenty-five-minute program.

As of this writing, our four programs combined—*Moody Church Hour, Songs in the Night,* and *Running to Win* (both versions)—are on about 1,700 outlets around the world every day, and we have good reason to believe that approximately a million people listen in the United States alone.

THE INTERNET

To reach beyond the neighborhood, The Moody Church has always been an early adopter of technology that can carry the gospel to a greater audience. So as the Internet began to expand, the church looked for ways to utilize this new technology to share the good news.

In 2003, live video streaming of the Sunday morning services began, and Moody Church Radio changed its name to the more inclusive Moody Church Media. *Moody Church Hour* and *Running to Win* broadcasts were hosted online for listeners all over the world, and sermons were available for download. One listener from China wrote:

I am a new Christian and am currently living and working in Shang-hai, China. There are times when I felt lost in my Bible reading, while listening to sermons in Mandarin.

One day I found out that there is free Internet access in my building and I immediately clicked on moodychurch.org. I like your sermons. They are so direct and true to the Scripture that it is a light in my walk with Christ. Your teaching is clear and that really helps me a lot in my Bible study and with a deeper understanding of the Scriptures. I would not be able to advance my walk with Christ had I not had access to all this via the Internet.

Continuing to embrace technological advancements, in 2011, The Moody Church launched a new website (moodychurch.org), which houses information for the various ministries and outreaches of the church and allows them to maintain their own blogs, videos and content to better serve the needs of their communities. Two years later, Moody Church Media launched a separate website (moodymedia.org) to provide easy access to my sermons and broadcasts along with resource materials from the church's 150-year history—free of cost to the user.

This online presence is a priority for the church as a way to bring sound Bible teaching to people who couldn't otherwise afford it or have access to it—the poor, people in developing nations, and particularly people living in closed countries where Christians are persecuted and missionaries are forbidden. To reach an even wider audience, social media was added into the mix, and a partnership with Trans World Radio's new venture, TWR360, allows us to provide people with access to Christian media resources, in their own language, using any media device.

The Moody Church has always been a light to the city and we continue to have a heart for the world. We are committed to use technology for the advancement of the gospel.

CHAPTER 15

Visiting the Sites of the Protestant Reformation

∿✦∿

W here God builds a church, the devil would build a chapel," observed Martin Luther in his *Table Talk*. And yes, it is true, that wherever God is at work, the Devil is there to try to usurp God's work and make it his own.

In the fall of 1970, Rebecca and I had settled into our apartment in Niles, a suburb of Chicago. She was working at Allstate Insurance to pay the bills while I was enrolled in Loyola University and also taking a class at Trinity Seminary taught by John Warwick Montgomery, the very man who encouraged me to turn my manuscript on situation ethics into a book. Montgomery told us he was leading a tour to the sites of the Reformation in Europe over the Christmas break. Since Rebecca and I had no children at the time and the cost was nominal ($550 per person covered airfare and hotels!), we decided to join the ninety other people for the trip. I didn't know this tour would awaken a desire to study the Reformation more carefully, and that I'd have the privilege of leading numerous tours to these same sites in later years.

The Cold War was still at its height back in 1970. We flew into Berlin, and from there we boarded three buses that would take us into East Germany where the Luther sites exist. As we approached the famous "Checkpoint Charlie" at the Berlin Wall and received permission to enter East Germany, it seemed to us that the Devil had built more than a chapel in the country where the Reformation was born. The presence of the East German guards, a glance at the Berlin Wall, and the visible sadness of those across the border convinced us that the Devil had erected not merely a chapel, but a castle on the very ground where the light of the gospel shone so brightly 450 years before.

We arrived in East Berlin just three days after Christmas. And now we would see the birthplaces of the Reformation firsthand. The East German government, though cautious about visitors, did grant permission for our visit through the diplomatic efforts of Dr. John Warwick Montgomery, who had made the trip on previous occasions. We were detained at the checkpoint for one hour and twenty-three minutes—it seemed longer. Our passports were checked and rechecked; we were told that our visa money had not arrived (although it was sent early in December). The red tape seemed endless. When we finally left the checkpoint at 4:24 p.m., darkness was already spreading over the city. Our first destination was Wittenberg, the center of Luther's Reformation activity.

It took two hours to cover the seventy kilometers from Berlin to Wittenberg. There was not much traffic on the autobahn, but it was snowing and the highway was slippery. For the last few miles, we took a winding two-lane road that led to Wittenberg. We peered through the bus window, straining to get a glimpse of the town, but we'd have to wait until morning to see it clearly.

We arrived at the "Golden Adler" (Golden Eagle) hotel where we would spend our first night behind the Iron Curtain. But before we went to bed, we received some firsthand information about what life was like in East Germany. One man recognized us as Americans and began to talk excitedly in broken English; he'd been in East Germany (which he referred to as a prison) for twenty years and longed for freedom. He envied us and reminded us of something we should never forget, namely, that if we didn't cherish our freedoms, we too might lose them.

A few minutes later, a woman asked if we would give her an American dollar in exchange for German marks. When I consented, she called her husband, and both of them jumped together for joy. She told me that she was a Christian. *"Christus ist in mein hertz,"* she said with sufficient boldness to make me believe she knew the true meaning of those words and was not ashamed of her faith. Could this woman be one to whom the torch of the Reformation had been passed? I wondered.

The next morning we walked the streets of Wittenberg and found the people to be extremely friendly. There was one striking characteristic of the town: dead silence. Even the children didn't shout or laugh. In the town square, directly in front of our hotel, were two statues, one of Martin Luther and the other of Philipp Melancthon.

Our tour guides, who spoke only broken English, were anxious to point out that Luther was honored in their cities for the simple reason that he overthrew the power of the church and resisted the pressure of organized religion. Thus the very man who stood for the infallibility of Holy Scripture and the man who did so much to recover the gospel, which had been lost to centuries of tradition was reinterpreted as a symbol of the strides made by the Communists who freed people from the bondage of religious oppression.

Of course, there was no mention of what Luther believed or what he turned toward when he left the established church. In Eisleben, where he was born, there's another heroic statue of him, but back in 1970 its prominence was shared by a statue of Vladimir Lenin. One wonders how Luther would react to such a tribute if he were alive!

THE WITTENBERG DOOR

The Castle Church where the *Ninety-Five Theses* were posted still stands essentially as it was in Luther's time, even though it was partially reconstructed in 1892. The wooden door was destroyed in a fire in 1760 and was replaced by an artistic bronze door upon which the *Theses* are engraved in Latin. Inside the church, Luther and Melancthon are buried along with the two Electors: Frederick the Wise and John the Constant.

Luther's tomb bears only a simple inscription: "Here lies the body of Luther, doctor of theology, who, on the 18th of February, 1546, in his native town Eisleben, succumbed to death after having lived 63 years, 2 months, 10 days." During the 1970s, Protestant services were still conducted in the church; ironically, a Communist youth organization also met in one of its towers.

However—and this is critical if we wish to understand modern Europe—when we visited the church in 2004, there was a service being conducted in German, and I stayed to listen. The pastor read from the Old Testament, the New Testament, and the Qur'an, and said that, "in this church we honor all three of the world's great religions!" All that was said with Luther buried fifteen feet from the pulpit!

Europe, as you know, has been paralyzed by political correctness, and thus Islam thrives as Christianity sharply declines. The great cathedrals of Europe, known as "the tombs of God," are increasingly being sold and turned into restaurants, high-end stores, and even mosques. Luther would not recognize the Germany he left behind.

There are two churches in Wittenberg. By nailing the *Ninety-Five Theses* in Latin to the door of the Castle Church (which was the university chapel), Luther had captured the attention of the scholars of Wittenberg. From the Castle Church we walked past the town square to the Town Church were Luther preached the gospel in German to the common people. In Luther's day there were no pews, and two thousand people, we were told, stood during the service, crammed into the sanctuary. It was frequently filled as people flocked from afar to hear him. The Town Church is properly called the original church of the Reformation; it was here that Communion was served to the laity on Christmas Day in 1521 for the first time in centuries.

THE SECRET OF LUTHER'S GREATNESS

On the outskirts of Eisenach, nestled deep in the forest is a castle that reveals to us the reason for Luther's greatness. After the Diet of Worms, Luther mysteriously disappeared. Many of his friends thought he was dead, but Luther was very much alive. He'd been condemned by both pope and emperor, and lest he be burned at the stake, Luther's prince, Frederick the Wise, gave instructions that Luther be hid. He was informed of the plan and reluctantly agreed to it. As he and a friend rode through the forest, armed horsemen jumped from the brush and dragged Luther to the ground. He was then put on a horse and led by circuitous roads through the woods until at dusk they arrived at the Wartburg Castle.

This was the castle we were anxious to visit. Our bus carried us to the bottom of the hill as far as the road allowed, and after a strenuous climb in the snow and ice, we arrived at the foot of the castle. The frost on the trees and the quietness of the falling snow made the castle appear like a fortress in a fairy tale. This ancient structure had already been in existence for four hundred years when Luther arrived. We saw the enormous room where monarchs, minstrels, and knights assembled. Here St. Elizabeth had left the relics of her holiness. Yet when Luther was here, he wasn't interested in these things. He had come as a fugitive; he was sought by the highest courts of the land.

We were directed to the room in which Luther lived for the ten months he was at the castle. It had only one window, a wooden floor, a small table, and a stove. It stood in sharp contrast to the other ornate and beautiful rooms in the castle. Even here Luther passed through mental anguish. As he lay down at night with the bats whirling about in the darkness, questions haunted him. "Are you the only one who is right? Has the church been wrong throughout the centuries?" The way in which Luther settled these questions is the secret of his greatness. He didn't analyze his existential experience to determine whether or not he was right. Nor did he think that truth could be determined by majority vote.

Just before he arrived at the castle he had boldly stated at the Diet of Worms, "I am bound by the Scriptures that I have adduced and my conscience has been taken captive by the Word of God; and I am neither able nor willing to recant, since it is neither safe nor right to act against conscience. God help me. Amen."

Further evidence of his view of *Sola Scriptura* abounds. He writes, "Therefore necessity compels us to run to the Bible with all the writings of the doctors, and thence to get our verdict and judgment upon them, for Scripture alone is the true overlord and master of all writings and doctrines on earth." Clearly, for Luther, Scripture alone was the basis for his authority; only the Word of God could determine whether he or the church was right. His conscience was taken captive by the Word of God.

A tradition developed about this room that Luther felt the presence of the Devil so strongly that he threw an inkwell at him! However, it's unlikely that he did that (tour guides used to rub some soot on the wall so tourists could see where the inkwell landed). In his *Table Talk* he said he "fought the devil with ink," almost certainly a reference to the fact that in this room he translated the entire New Testament into German in just ten weeks.

The New Testament Luther translated and the books he wrote in that room are the "ink" that fought the Devil. For Luther, the gospel was the source of power and freedom. The torch lit by him was the Word of God made available to all people.

The secret of his courage was simply the power of the Word of God.

LEADING TOURS TO THE SITES OF THE REFORMATION

I credit that first tour with lighting a fire within me for the history of the Reformation (I'm currently writing a book on the topic). It was unrealistic for me to lead tours when our children were young, so Rebecca and I didn't lead our first tour to these sites until 1992, and we've returned numerous times since. I enjoy helping people understand the high price that many people have paid for maintaining the integrity of the gospel against opposition—in Luther's case, he had to buck centuries of tradition.

On our tours we not only visit the Luther sites, but usually also go to Calvin's Church in Geneva and Huldrych Zwingli's *Grossmünster* in Zurich. What history textbook can compare to actually standing on the banks of the Limatt River in Zurich and pointing out the exact spot where Felix Manse was forcibly drowned? And believe it or not—his mentor, Zwingli, was on the shore watching his former student drowning and approved of it!

Manse's crime was that he repudiated infant baptism and was baptized as an adult upon profession of his faith. The Zurich city council decreed that anyone who practiced believer's baptism was to be put to death by fire, drowning, or sword. It's reported that when Manse was pushed into the water on a raft that was then overturned, Zwingli is to have said sarcastically, "If he wishes to go under the water, then let him go under!" [Since he wanted to go under the water (believer's baptism) then let us put him under the water (let him be drowned).]

No one can stand on that riverbank and remain unmoved.

A PERSONAL EXPERIENCE

In the year 2010, we were able to visit the church in Eisleben where Luther preached his last sermon. If you're acquainted with the churches in Europe, you'll know that the pulpit is usually perched high up (the symbolism is that the preached Word is above the choir loft and the people). And, to make sure that tourists don't go up the spiral staircase to the pulpit, a rope is tied across the entrance of the stairway.

But when I explained that I was a pastor from the United States, the proprietor graciously untied the rope and let me speak from the pulpit—yes, the very pulpit where Luther preached his last sermon! And as providence (along with careful planning) would have it, I had the text of Luther's last sermon with me.

And so I preached a few paragraphs of Luther's last sermon in the same pulpit where he preached it. He preached this sermon on February 15, 1546. His text was Matthew 11:26: "At that time Jesus declared, 'I thank you, Father, Lord of heaven and earth, that you have hidden these things from the wise and the understanding and have revealed them to little children; yes, Father, for such was your gracious will.'"

I quote a few paragraphs, reminding us of the relevance of his words for today. I have made a few edits in these paragraphs for the sake of clarity.

This is a fine gospel and it has a lot in it. Let us talk about part of it now, covering as much as we can and as God gives us grace.

The Lord here praises and extols His heavenly Father for having

hidden these things from the wise and understanding. That is, He did
not make His gospel known to the wise and understanding, but to in-
fants and children who cannot speak and preach and be wise. Thus He
indicates that He is opposed to the wise and understanding and dearly
loves those who are like young children.

But to the world it is very foolish and offensive that God should be
opposed to the wise and condemn them, when, after all, we have the
idea that God could not reign if He did not have wise and understand-
ing people to help Him. But the wise and understanding in the world
so contrive things that God cannot be favorable and good to them. For
they are always exerting themselves; they do things in the Christian
church the way they want to. Everything that God does they must
improve, so that there is no poorer, more insignificant and despised
disciple on earth than God. He must be everybody's pupil, everybody
wants to be His teacher.

A fine governance it must be when the children want to rule their
father and mother, and the fools and simpletons see themselves as the
wise people. You see, this is the reason why the wise and understanding
are condemned everywhere in the Scriptures.

The devil has slobbered us with fools. . . They imagine that because
they are in the government and are higher-ups they must surely be wise.
So the pope, too, wants to be a very wise man, indeed, the wisest of the
wise, simply because he has a high position and claims to be the head
of the church; whereupon the devil so puffs him up that he [the pope]
imagines that whatever he says and does is pure divine wisdom and
everybody must accept and obey it, and nobody should ask whether it is
God's Word or not.

But this, God will not tolerate. He has no intention of being a
pupil; they are to be the pupils. They who are rulers in the church think
they see more deeply into the Scriptures than other people. Therefore

God brings them to terrible destruction; for He will not and cannot, nor should He, tolerate it. He is the eternal wisdom and He knows very well what He wishes to do or not to do.

Lo, this means that the wise of this world are rejected, that we may learn not to think ourselves wise . . . but to cling only to Christ's Word and come to Him, as He so lovingly invites us to do, and say: Thou alone art my beloved Lord and Master, I am Thy disciple.

This and much more might be said concerning this Gospel, but I am too weak and we shall let it go at that.[3]

Luther preached for what must have been a total of about thirty to thirty-five minutes, and in conclusion admitted that he was "too weak" to say more. He left the church, walked across the street to his room, took sick, and died a few days later.

The legacy of Martin Luther reminds us that each generation is called upon to live out the gospel and preach it to all who will hear. We have been given the baton and we must pass it on to those who follow us.

The privilege of such educational travel is another of God's gifts to me and my family. Thanks to the prayers of many, I have been blessed.

CHAPTER 16

Passing the Baton

✻

Preaching has fallen on hard times.

There was a time in US history when pastors/preachers were respected in their community. Politicians curried their favor and newspapers consulted them about matters of culture, morality, and yes, even politics. There were wrongs that needed to be corrected and sins that needed to be exposed. Preaching was expected to challenge culture, not merely reflect it.

For the most part, all of that has changed.

For some people, the very idea that a man should stand behind a pulpit (even if it is made of Plexiglas) and tell others what they should think or believe is repugnant. To enter into dialogue, the argument goes, would be so much more respectful. After all, we should take everyone's opinion into account, rather than just sit and listen to one "man of God" tell us what God thinks about us, the culture, and the events shaping our world.

Furthermore, for many, the Bible itself is socially repressive. Its view of slavery, women, and homosexuality is seen to be a throwback to a primitive culture that has become an embarrassment to moderns. I'm sure then-Senator Barack Obama spoke for many when, in a 2006 speech, he talked mockingly about his approach to the Bible:

"Which passages of Scripture should guide our public policy? Should we go with Leviticus, which suggests slavery is okay and that eating shellfish is abomination? How about Deuteronomy, which suggests stoning your child if he strays from the faith? Or should we just stick to the Sermon on the Mount—a passage that is so radical that it's doubtful that our own Defense Department would survive its application?"[4]

Just so, many people today superficially dismiss the Bible as irrelevant, anachronistic, and embarrassing. Our "sound bite" culture is not given to thoughtful evaluations and historical perspective. All they need to hear is one carefully chosen Bible verse they don't like to give them a reason to dismiss it all.

Frankie Schaeffer, the son of the late Francis and Edith Schaeffer, tells evangelicals that we had better get on board with matters such as same-sex marriage or we'll be rejected and marginalized. Years ago, Frankie abandoned the faith of his parents and decided to opt for a completely liberal social and political agenda that is the dominant trend of the times. He wrote to evangelicals warning us that we'd better get with the culture rather than being known for opposing it. Our evangelical schools, he said, will be without students and our churches empty.

In addition to perceived irrelevancy, other challenges also lie before us. What can we say about the health-and-wealth charlatans on television who tell us that we'll have a great spiritual breakthrough if only we'll send them a large financial gift? Just survey the religious channels in your area, and you'll find outrageous claims being made by so-called evangelists who are constantly telling people to "plant a seed," and the larger the gift to them, the larger the harvest. No wonder the New Testament repeatedly teaches that one of the signs of a false prophet is material gain.

Preachers have only themselves to thank for adding to the pervasive distrust of biblical authority. The high-profile scandals that have rocked the evangelical community in the past several decades have eroded the image of a pastor as a man to be trusted and believed. As for the Catholic Church, its scandals of priests having sex with altar boys have caused millions to leave their churches, wanting nothing to do with institutional Christianity of any kind.

And yet, despite all this, I still believe in preaching.

My predecessor at The Moody Church, Dr. Warren Wiersbe, used to say, "There is no substitute for the man of God taking the Word of God by the power of the Spirit of God and proclaiming it to the people of God." Agreed.

If my epitaph would read, "He loved preaching the gospel," I would be abundantly satisfied.

What kind of preachers do we need?

PREACHERS WHO ARE CALLED TO PREACH

First, we need preachers who are *called to preach*. We don't hear much today about the calling to preach the gospel. We've been told that emphasizing a call to the ministry exaggerates the distinction between clergy and laity. To say that some Christians are called to specific ministries while others aren't seems contrary to the biblical teaching that each member of the body of Christ has significance. All believers, we are told, are "called" to something. Faithfulness in all vocations is important.

Despite the fact that "the call" means different things to different people, I believe there is a call to be a preacher. It is more than simply being gifted for ministry, and even more than just a desire to preach or teach. Charles Bridges has a point when he says that ministerial failure can sometimes be traced "to the very threshold of the entrance to the work."

The late J. Oswald Sanders was right when he said that the supernatural nature of the church demands a leadership that rises above the human. He wrote, "If the world is to hear the church's voice today, leaders are needed who are authoritative, spiritual, and sacrificial . . . Spiritual leaders are not elected, appointed, or created by synods or church assemblies. God alone makes them."[5] Charles Spurgeon and Billy Graham, along with hundreds of other preachers, have said that they chose the ministry only because God chose them for it.

I'm disturbed by those who preach and teach without a sense of calling. Those who consider the ministry to be one choice among many tend to have horizontal vision. They lack the urgency of Paul, who said, "Necessity is laid upon me." John Jowett says, "If we lose the sense of wonder of our commission, we shall become like common traders in a common market, babbling about common wares."[6]

Let me risk my own definition of a call: *God's call is an inner conviction given by the Holy Spirit and confirmed by the Word of God and the Body of Christ.*

Notice the three parts to the definition. First, it's an inner conviction. Feelings and hunches come and go. They may be based on impressions we had as children when we romanticized the idea of becoming a missionary. Or maybe we idolized the role of a pastor.

But a God-given compulsion is not deterred by obstacles. It gives us the single-mindedness needed for effective ministry. Some of us have had this conviction from our youth; others had a growing sense of urgency as they studied the Bible; others perhaps had a less distinct, but no less sure, sense of direction. But the bottom line is the same: all had a strong desire to preach, join a mission team, or perhaps train others in the Word.

Of course, we don't all have to be called the same way. Circumstances and temperaments vary. Some have been called to preach when were very young; others in later life. A person may sense no call at all until encouraged by discerning members of the body of Christ. Yet despite those differences, there's a sense of purpose. Yes, "Woe to me if I do not preach the gospel!"

The Word of God must confirm our call. We have to ask whether a person has the qualifications listed in 1 Timothy 3. Is he mature? Does he have the gifts needed? Has he labored in the Word of God and in doctrine? Or might he have disqualified himself through moral or doctrinal compromise? Character and doctrine are indispensable ingredients.

The leaders of the church in Antioch were ministering to the Lord and fasting when the Holy Spirit said, "Set apart for me Barnabas and Saul for the work to which I have called them" (Acts 13:2). The body enables its members to find their spiritual gifts and is a testing ground for further ministry. I personally felt "called" to preach when I was a teenager, but if the body of Christ had not confirmed my conviction, I could not have pursued the ministerial path.

Our response to God's call should be one of amazed humility. Every one of us should have a sense of authority and boldness. We should be characterized by unusual earnestness and diligence in study and prayer. Jowett perhaps overstated it only slightly when he wrote, "The call of the Eternal must ring through the rooms of his soul as clearly as the sound of the morning-bell rings through the valleys of Switzerland, calling the peasants to early prayer and praise."[7] Luther warned, "Wert thou wiser than Solomon and David, and yet were thou not called, flee the ministry like hell and the devil . . . if God hath need of thee, he will know how to call thee."

PREACHERS WITH CONVICTION

Good preaching is *rooted in Scripture* and applied first to the life and experience of the preacher and then to the congregation. I sometimes tell young preachers to remember that the Bible was not written to be studied. They are surprised of course to hear me say that, but I want them to grasp my point. Then I add, "The Bible was written to change your life; studying it is simply a means to getting a better grasp of its message, but the goal should always be personal and corporate transformation."

Having been called, we need a sense of conviction—*a fire in our bones*. What is too often lacking today, I believe, is a lack of passion on the part of the preacher. There often is no sense of urgency of the message. I'm not talking about loud preaching; I personally don't respond favorably to those preachers who I feel are hollering at me. But I will listen to someone preaching in sincerity, someone who deeply believes what he says not just with his head but with his heart. Perhaps the best word is *earnestness*.

There is such a thing as head-to-head preaching; when the sermon is over, people say, "That was interesting," or "I've never thought of that before." But there is also heart-to-heart preaching; there is preaching that comes from *both* the mind and heart.

Whenever I prepare a message I ask myself, "Why should someone's life be changed forever because of this message?" If I can't answer that question, I can't justify preaching the sermon. A message must aim for the transformation of life.

In recent years, rather than preaching through books of the Bible, I've chosen to preach on themes, so that the series of messages is connected around these themes. Of course, this is also expository preaching; each sermon is best described as topical exposition. I choose various passages that relate to an overall theme, and I preach these messages in sequence.

For example, I've recently preached a series on prophecy, the power of a clear conscience, the invisible (spiritual) world, and sexual purity in a media-saturated culture.

Effective preaching is taking the Bible in its context and applying it to ourselves and then our hearers. Richard Baxter is quoted as saying, "We must preach as a dying man preaching to dying men."

PREACHERS WHO ARE BALANCED IN CONTENT

Many preachers concentrate only on the more positive themes of Scripture, the love of God, grace, Jesus helps you be a better father, have a better family, etc. And they shy away from the controversial cultural issues. There is in evangelicalism such an emphasis on grace that you'd never think that God hates sin and plans to judge it in multiple ways.

In previous generations, the law was preached, then when people were convicted of their sin, grace was offered to them. But today, grace is being offered up front, even before people are convinced that they need it. Jonathan Edwards, I fear, would not recognize today's church.

This deserves a longer discussion, but I believe that preachers should not avoid preaching "the whole counsel of God," which would include subjects such as same-sex marriage, the sacredness of human life, the danger of false prophets, racism, God's judgment on sin, and the doctrine of hell, to name but a few. We must lovingly tackle sensitive topics such as sexual abuse, addictions, and even relevant political issues. A congregation should be able to look to its pastor to help them see the world through a biblical lens. We must have informed, winsome, but also *courageous* preaching.

PREACHERS WITH INTEGRITY

Finally, we need to preach with *integrity*. That is, we dare not give the impression that we have it all together, that pastors no longer struggle with sin, or that our lives are free from the vicissitudes of our congregation. Professor Howard Hendricks told us students that, "We should never give the impression that we go to heaven every evening and return in the morning!" As a general rule, our personal illustrations—and yes, I think we should use personal references with discretion—should not always be ones in which we are the hero of the story.

It all comes down to this: I believe preaching that exposes human need and exalts Christ as the answer to that need—that kind of preaching will never go out of style or out of vogue. Spurgeon said that he didn't know what heaven would actually be like, but he suspected he'd have an experience that was akin to those moments when he was preaching and the Holy Spirit gave him a special anointing. Such Spirit-filled preaching is sorely needed in our media-driven, pleasure-seeking, and ofttimes superficial generation.

PREACHERS, GRAVEYARDS, AND RESURRECTIONS

"Lord, help me to think of ways to enable my students to understand how desperately we need to depend on You for the preaching of the gospel!"

I prayed that prayer while driving home from teaching at Trinity Seminary in Deerfield, Illinois. For several years I taught a class in preaching at the seminary, and I longed to get my point across that *without the work of God, all preaching is in vain and no one will be blessed or saved.*

Immediately after the prayer, an idea came to mind. "Why don't I take the students to a cemetery and have them preach to the dead? That would help them understand what it was like to preach to people who were 'dead in trespasses and sins.'"

The next week, I left early for my class and decided to stop at a restaurant in town to see if I could find someone who knew where the cemetery was located. I stopped at the first restaurant I saw, and as I opened the door, a couple emerged. Somewhat apologetically, I asked them if they knew where the Deerfield cemetery was. "Just ask this man," the woman said, pointing to her husband. "He's the caretaker of the cemetery!" If I had any doubt that God was in on this idea, it vanished at that moment. The man told me where it was and yes, I could take students into the cemetery.

That day, I asked the students to join me at the cemetery, and when they all arrived, I gave them their assignment. I explained that the Bible described people as "dead in their trespasses and sins" and that to get a feel for what it's like to preach to the lost, they should each choose a tombstone and preach to that particular person and ask him/her to rise from the dead! They thought I had taken leave of my mind and just stared at me.

So, if they wouldn't do it, I would. I chose a grave marked Jonathan (died 1914), leaned over, and shouted to him to rise from the dead. Then I waited for a resurrection. Thankfully, my command wasn't honored! A student told me later that he backed away and was ready to run, fearing that the dead man might actually rise!

Then I made my point. How foolish it is for us to think that we can raise the dead. Just so, it's foolish to think that our preaching can save the lost—unless of course, God were to choose to perform a resurrection. When we preach the gospel, we're expecting the dead to rise, the deaf to hear, and the blind to see. Jesus said, "As the Father raises the dead and gives them life, so also the Son gives life to whom He will." Each conversion is a resurrection.

After expounding on several passages, I ended by turning to Ezekiel 37 where we read that the prophet was asked to preach to dry bones—an assignment we can all identify with. Foolish indeed! And yet, when he began to preach, the bones came together, God breathed life into them, and the dry bones lived. Just so, God can and does raise the spiritually dead even as we preach. After this exposition of Scripture, we all knelt on the grass in the cemetery affirming our complete and utter dependence on God in the proclamation of the gospel.

In the years that God may still give to me, I want to devote myself to helping young pastors with encouragement and instruction. I want to inspire them to believe in preaching, to help them see that modern technology must serve the preacher's sermon and not control it. To use a video clip of a movie to make a point might be appropriate if it supports the sermon, but it should neither substitute nor detract from the preacher's passion and heart.

God is still calling men to "Preach the Word." As the old adage used to say, "If God calls you to be a preacher, don't stoop to become a king."

As I face the future, fully aware that most of my years have already been spent, I pray that I will be able to say with Paul, "But I do not account my life of any value nor as precious to myself, if only I may finish my course and the ministry that I received from the Lord Jesus, to testify to the gospel of the grace of God" (Acts 20:24).

Amen. And amen.

NOTES

1. Austin Miles, *Setting the Captives Free: Victims of the Church Tell Their Stories* (Buffalo, New York: Prometheus Books, 1990), 196, 197.

2. Stephen T. Um and Justin Buzzard, *Why Cities Matter to God, the Culture, and the Church* (Wheaton, IL: Crossway; 2013), 90.

3. Martin Luther, *Luther's Works, Sermons*, vol. 51; J. J. Pelikan, H. C. Oswald, and H. T. Lehman, eds. (Philadelphia: Fortress press, 1999, c1959).

4. http://religion.blogs.cnn.com/2012/10/21/to-some-obama-is-the-wrong-kind-of-christian/comment-page-1/.

5. J. Oswald Sanders, *Spiritual Leadership* (Chicago: Moody Publishers, 1994), 18.

6. John Jowett, *The Preacher: His Life and Work* (Grand Rapids: Baker, 1968), 21.

7. Ibid., 12.

ACKNOWLEDGMENTS

This book has been a community project. Special thanks goes to my wife, Rebecca, who gave me some valuable editorial advice and without whose cooperation and encouragement our combined stories could not have been written. Without her at my side my life would have taken an entirely different turn and I would be—who knows where!? Warm thanks to our daughters, Lori, Lynn, and Lisa for their input, and especially to Lori for the many hours spent locating the pictures and preparing them for publication.

The team at Moody Publishers has been superb in their advice and encouragement. Duane Sherman, Betsey Newenhuyse, and Erik Peterson, you eagerly embraced this project and kept the vision of this book alive in my heart. Thank you for your willingness to walk with me through the steps that have led to its publication. I am truly humbled by your commitment to me and my writing ministry. "For God is not so unjust as to overlook your work and love that you showed for his sake in serving the saints, as you still do" (Hebrews 6:10).

MORE BOOKS BY ERWIN W. LUTZER

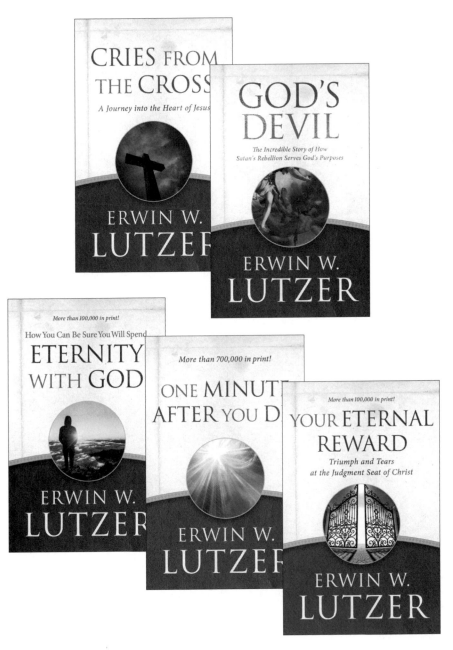

MOODY
Publishers™

From the Word to Life

ONE MINUTE
AFTER YOU DIE

- Book
- Study Guide
- DVD

MOODY
Publishers™

*From the Word **to** Life*

MOODYMEDIA.ORG
DECADES OF TEACHING
AT YOUR FINGERTIPS

- **Ask**
- **Listen**
- **Download**
- **Share**
- **Read**
- **Shop**

Moody
Church
media

Visit **moodymedia.org** to download sermons free of charge, listen to radio broadcasts, and read articles by Dr. Erwin Lutzer.

Moody Church Media is listener supported. Connect with us at 1.800.215.5001 or media@moodychurch.org.

MOODY
Radio™

From the Word **to Life**

Moody Radio produces and delivers compelling programs filled with biblical insights and creative expressions of faith that help you take the next step in your relationship with Christ.

You can hear Moody Radio on 36 stations and more than 1,500 radio outlets across the U.S. and Canada. Or listen on your smartphone with the Moody Radio app!

www.moodyradio.org

109 Every we can't su g. 1
Ws Secres
270
208

170 Hrbot to Thsats 170
170 191 193
191 X 152 162

38 N Gen-Chgo Towa
Nobu
139
141

Jdug 94
199 LScsJouls 151 14 Oct